Approaches to learning and teaching

Global Perspectives

a toolkit for international teachers

Keely Laycock

Series Editors: Paul Ellis and Lauren Harris

CAMBRIDGE
UNIVERSITY PRESS

University Printing House, Cambridge CB2 8BS, United Kingdom

One Liberty Plaza, 20th Floor, New York, NY 10006, USA

477 Williamstown Road, Port Melbourne, VIC 3207, Australia

4843/24, 2nd Floor, Ansari Road, Daryaganj, Delhi – 110002, India

79 Anson Road, #06–04/06, Singapore 079906

Cambridge University Press is part of the University of Cambridge.

It furthers the University's mission by disseminating knowledge in the pursuit of education, learning and research at the highest international levels of excellence.

www.cambridge.org
Information on this title: www.cambridge.org/9781316638750 (Paperback)

© Cambridge International Examinations 2017

First published 2017

20 19 18 17 16 15 14 13 12 11 10 9 8 7 6 5 4 3 2 1

Printed in Great Britain by CPI Group (UK) Ltd, Croydon CR0 4YY

A catalogue record for this publication is available from the British Library

ISBN 978-1-316-63875-0 Paperback

Contents

Acknowledgements

The authors and publishers acknowledge the following sources of copyright material and are grateful for the permissions granted.

Cover bgblue/Getty Images; Fig 3.2 Flashpop/Getty images; Fig 5.2 Phil Boorman/Getty Images; Lesson idea 5.7 Fig 5.4 Margo Silver/ Getty Images, Fig 5.5 Alexei Novikov/Shutterstock; Fig 6.2 Johner Images/Getty Images; Lesson idea 6.5 Fig 6.1Alexei Novikov/ Shutterstock, Fig 6.2 Shutterstock/Piero Cruciatti, Fig 6.3 Paula Bronstein/Getty Images, Fig 6.4Vaclav Volrab/Shutterstock; Fig 8.2 Gary Waters/Getty Images; Chapter 8 `Use of visuals' text B images – top Alexei Novikov/Shutterstock; centre David Goddard/Getty Images; bottom Joe Raedle/Getty Images; Lesson idea 8.5 Andy Rouse/Getty Images; Lesson idea 10.4 Fig 10.1Ron Nickel/Getty Images; Lesson idea 11.6 tl Andrew Rowat/Getty Images, tr Gerhard Joren/LightRocket via Getty Images, bl Rhapsode/Getty Images, br Ahmed Ibrahim/Anadolu Agency/Getty Images

Introduction to the series by the editors

1

1 Approaches to learning and teaching Global Perspectives

This series of books is the result of close collaboration between Cambridge University Press and Cambridge International Examinations, both departments of the University of Cambridge. The books are intended as a companion guide for teachers, to supplement your learning and provide you with extra resources for the lessons you are planning. Their focus is deliberately not syllabus-specific, although occasional reference has been made to programmes and qualifications. We want to invite you to set aside for a while assessment objectives and grading, and take the opportunity instead to look in more depth at how you teach your subject and how you motivate and engage with your students.

The themes presented in these books are informed by evidence-based research into what works to improve students' learning and pedagogical best practices. To ensure that these books are first and foremost practical resources, we have chosen not to include too many academic references, but we have provided some suggestions for further reading.

We have further enhanced the books by asking the authors to create accompanying lesson ideas. These are described in the text and can be found in a dedicated space online. We hope the books will become a dynamic and valid representation of what is happening now in learning and teaching in the context in which you work.

Our organisations also offer a wide range of professional development opportunities for teachers. These range from syllabus- and topic-specific workshops and large-scale conferences to suites of accredited qualifications for teachers and school leaders. Our aim is to provide you with valuable support, to build communities and networks, and to help you both enrich your own teaching methodology and evaluate its impact on your students.

Each of the books in this series follows a similar structure. In the first chapter, we have asked our authors to consider the essential elements of their subject, the main concepts that might be covered in a school curriculum, and why these are important. The next chapter gives you a brief guide on how to interpret a syllabus or subject guide, and how to plan a programme of study. The authors will encourage you to think too about what is not contained in a syllabus and how you can pass on your own passion for the subject you teach.

The main body of the text takes you through those aspects of learning and teaching which are widely recognised as important. We would like to stress that there is no single recipe for excellent teaching, and that different schools, operating in different countries and cultures, will have strong traditions that should be respected. There is a growing consensus, however, about some important practices and approaches that need to be adopted if students are going to fulfil their potential and be prepared for modern life.

In the common introduction to each of these chapters we look at what the research says and the benefits and challenges of particular approaches. Each author then focuses on how to translate theory into practice in the context of their subject, offering practical lesson ideas and teacher tips. These chapters are not mutually exclusive but can be read independently of each other and in whichever order suits you best. They form a coherent whole but are presented in such a way that you can dip into the book when and where it is most convenient for you to do so.

The final two chapters are common to all the books in this series and are not written by the subject authors. Schools and educational organisations are increasingly interested in the impact that classroom practice has on student outcomes. We have therefore included an exploration of this topic and some practical advice on how to evaluate the success of the learning opportunities you are providing for your students. The book then closes with some guidance on how to reflect on your teaching and some avenues you might explore to develop your own professional learning.

We hope you find these books accessible and useful. We have tried to make them conversational in tone so you feel we are sharing good practice rather than directing it. Above all, we hope that the books will inspire you and enable you to think in more depth about how you teach and how your students learn.

Paul Ellis and Lauren Harris

Series Editors

2 | Purpose and context

International research into educational effectiveness tells us that student achievement is influenced most by what teachers do in classrooms. In a world of rankings and league tables we tend to notice performance, not preparation, yet the product of education is more than just examinations and certification. Education is also about the formation of effective learning habits that are crucial for success within and beyond the taught curriculum.

The purpose of this series of books is to inspire you as a teacher to reflect on your practice, try new approaches and better understand how to help your students learn. We aim to help you develop your teaching so that your students are prepared for the next level of their education as well as life in the modern world.

This book will encourage you to examine the processes of learning and teaching, not just the outcomes. We will explore a variety of teaching strategies to enable you to select which is most appropriate for your students and the context in which you teach. When you are making your choice, involve your students: all the ideas presented in this book will work best if you engage your students, listen to what they have to say, and consistently evaluate their needs.

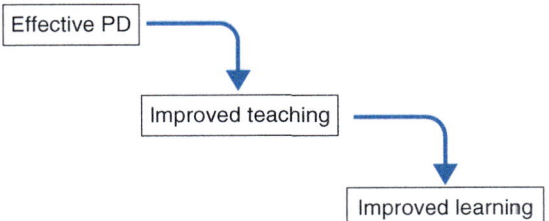

Cognitive psychologists, coaches and sports writers have noted how the aggregation of small changes can lead to success at the highest level. As teachers, we can help our students make marginal gains by guiding them in their learning, encouraging them to think and talk about how they are learning, and giving them the tools to monitor their success. If you take care of the learning, the performance will take care of itself.

When approaching an activity for the first time, or revisiting an area of learning, ask yourself if your students know how to:

* approach a new task and plan which strategies they will use
* monitor their progress and adapt their approach if necessary
* look back and reflect on how well they did and what they might do differently next time.

2 Approaches to learning and teaching Global Perspectives

Effective learners understand that learning is an active process. We need to challenge and stretch our students and enable them to interrogate, analyse and evaluate what they see and hear. Consider whether your students:

* challenge assumptions and ask questions
* try new ideas and take intellectual risks
* devise strategies to overcome any barriers to their learning that they encounter.

As we discuss in the chapters on **Active learning** and **Metacognition**, it is our role as teachers to encourage these practices with our students so that they become established routines. We can help students review their own progress as well as getting a snapshot ourselves of how far they are progressing by using some of the methods we explore in the chapter on **Assessment for Learning**.

Students often view the subject lessons they are attending as separate from each other, but they can gain a great deal if we encourage them to take a more holistic appreciation of what they are learning. This requires not only understanding how various concepts in a subject fit together, but also how to make connections between different areas of knowledge and how to transfer skills from one discipline to another. As our students successfully integrate disciplinary knowledge, they are better able to solve complex problems, generate new ideas and interpret the world around them.

In order for students to construct an understanding of the world and their significance in it, we need to lead students into thinking habitually about why a topic is important on a personal, local and global scale. Do they realise the implications of what they are learning and what they do with their knowledge and skills, not only for themselves but also for their neighbours and the wider world? To what extent can they recognise and express their own perspective as well as the perspectives of others? We will consider how to foster local and global awareness, as well as personal and social responsibility, in the chapter on **Global thinking**.

As part of the learning process, some students will discover barriers to their learning: we need to recognise these and help students to overcome them. Even students who regularly meet success face their own challenges. We have all experienced barriers to our own learning at some point in our lives and should be able as teachers to empathise and share our own methods for dealing with these. In the chapter on **Inclusive education** we discuss how to make learning accessible for everyone and how to ensure that all students receive the instruction and support they need to succeed as learners.

Some students are learning through the medium of English when it is not their first language, while others may struggle to understand subject jargon even if they might otherwise appear fluent. For all students, whether they are learning through their first language or an additional language, language is a vehicle for learning. It is through language that students access the content of the lesson and communicate their ideas. So, as teachers, it is our responsibility to make sure that language isn't a barrier to learning. In the chapter on **Language awareness** we look at how teachers can pay closer attention to language to ensure that all students can access the content of a lesson.

Alongside a greater understanding of what works in education and why, we as teachers can also seek to improve how we teach and expand the tools we have at our disposal. For this reason, we have included a chapter in this book on **Teaching with digital technologies**, discussing what this means for our classrooms and for us as teachers. Institutes of higher education and employers want to work with students who are effective communicators and who are information literate. Technology brings both advantages and challenges and we invite you to reflect on how to use it appropriately.

This book has been written to help you think harder about the impact of your teaching on your students' learning. It is up to you to set an example for your students and to provide them with opportunities to celebrate success, learn from failure and, ultimately, to succeed.

We hope you will share what you gain from this book with other teachers and that you will be inspired by the ideas that are presented here. We hope that you will encourage your school leaders to foster a positive environment that allows both you and your students to meet with success and to learn from mistakes when success is not immediate. We hope too that this book can help in the creation and continuation of a culture where learning and teaching are valued and through which we can discover together what works best for each and every one of our students.

3

The nature of the subject and key considerations

The place of Global Perspectives in the curriculum

Global Perspectives is a wonderful subject that allows students to explore and question the world they live in, asking questions like, 'How do my actions impact my community?' and 'Why are animals and plant life so important to humanity?' It is a relatively new school subject, in comparison with traditional subjects like Mathematics. Sciences, Languages, and so on. It has often been classed as part of Humanities or Social Sciences, along with History and Geography or Business Studies and Enterprise. It is unique in that it develops skills through the use of global topics. These are many and varied, and include topics such as globalisation, humans and other species, conflict and peace, and education for all.

As well as helping students with other school subjects and activities, studying Global Perspectives helps prepare them to take their place as global citizens as they enter further education and the world of work.

Teacher Tip

Global Perspectives topics are designed to relate to current world events, which are of interest to students and teachers alike. Just take a look at an issue in the news and see which global topic it relates to. For example, you are likely to come across issues within the topics of fuel and energy, globalisation and migration.

LESSON IDEA 3.1: GLOBAL TOPICS

As a starter activity, find a 10–15 minute (maximum) news clip on the internet and ask students to identify the global topic. Choose from migration, fuel and energy, conflict and peace, or globalisation. Ask them to explain how this global topic is relevant to them.

Who are Global Perspectives teachers?

Global Perspectives teachers stem from a wide range of disciplines. As a trained Languages teacher, I was always pretty well equipped to develop communication skills; reading, writing, listening and speaking. I just needed a few ideas to develop the other skills – ideas that this book will give you. As someone who is passionate about the active learning approach (see Chapter 5 **Active learning** for more about this) and collaborative learning, my way of teaching seemed to match well with that needed for developing students' skills in Global Perspectives. These skills are research, analysis, evaluation, reflection, collaboration and communication. You will be hearing a lot more about these terms in this book so don't worry if you're not too sure about them at the moment.

What's important is that you:

- have a genuine interest in what's happening in the world around you
- want to instil in students a sense of their own place in this world
- are willing to learn new skills, be creative and promote an active role for students in their own learning.

Teacher Tip

Let's take another look at those key skills that Global Perspectives develops. See if you can come up with a definition for each skill before looking at the one given. You could cover the definitions and then check your understanding by uncovering them.

Skill	Definition
Research	Investigation into and study of materials and sources in order to establish facts and reach new conclusions
Analysis	Breaking down of a topic into issues and exploring the causes and consequences of these issues

Evaluation	Assessment of the strengths and weaknesses of something
Reflection	Serious thought or consideration about something you have done or something that has happened
Communication	Transferring information from one place to another, either by using spoken or written texts or by non-verbal means
Collaboration	Working together with others

☑ **LESSON IDEA ONLINE 3.2: MOBILE PHONE ACTIVITY**
Use this lesson idea as a way of getting your students to start thinking about the skills that they will be developing during their Global Perspectives studies.

The contribution made by Global Perspectives to the curriculum

Effective teaching and learning in Global Perspectives requires teachers and students to understand the purpose of the subject and how it contributes to the curriculum as a whole. Figure 3.1 highlights the contribution that Global Perspectives makes to the curriculum, both its distinctive contribution and how it contributes to the wider curriculum. Not only does the study of Global Perspectives help students with other school subjects and activities, but it also helps prepare them to take their place as global citizens as they enter further education and the world of work.

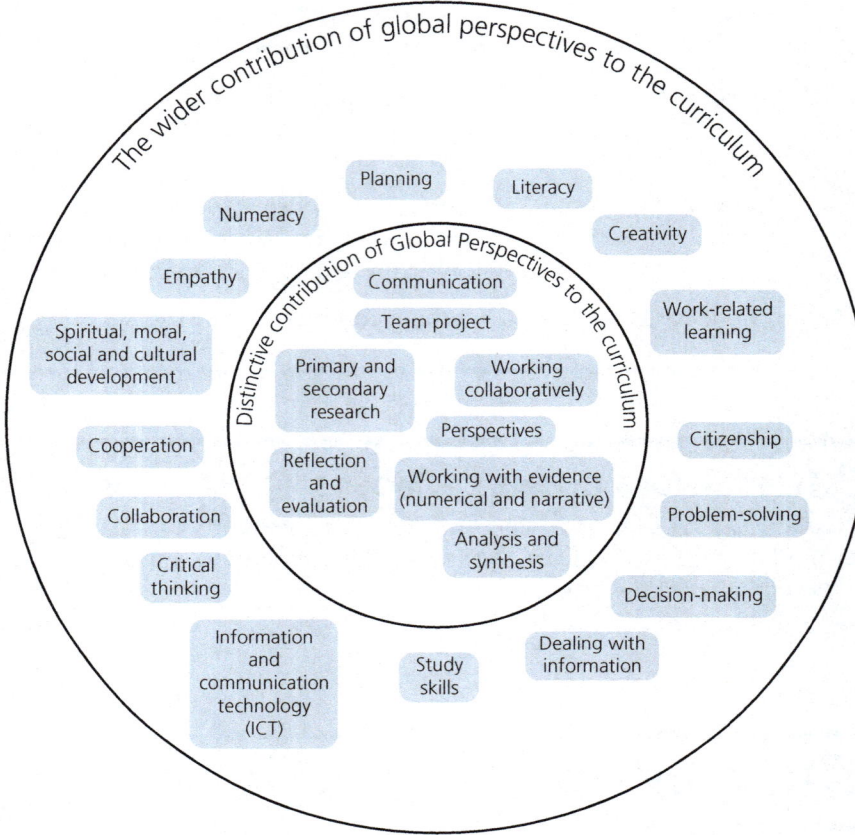

Figure 3.1: The contribution made by Global Perspectives to the curriculum.

Teacher Tip

It's a good idea to spend some time reflecting on the contribution that Global Perspectives makes to the curriculum by asking yourself the following three questions:

1 Which of the wider contributions that Global Perspectives makes to the curriculum do I think is the most important, and why do I think this?
2 Do my lessons enable all students to access the distinctive contributions that Global Perspectives makes to the curriculum?
3 Do I need to provide further opportunities for students to be able to make the most of the distinctive contributions that Global Perspectives offers?

You will have noticed that reflection is one of the skills that Global Perspectives develops. Throughout my experience, I have met many teachers who say that they have little time to reflect, but some, including me, find that it's certainly worth making time for. Developing your own reflective practice will help when it comes to developing your students' ability to reflect during their Global Perspectives course.

Effective teaching and learning in Global Perspectives

Before starting to teach any subject, most teachers ask themselves the following three questions:

1   What am I teaching?
2   What are my students learning?
3   How is my students' learning being assessed?

To get a better idea of what Global Perspectives is all about, let's look at each of these questions in turn.

What am I teaching?

While most subjects have subject-specific content that is covered throughout the course of study, Global Perspectives is a subject that focuses on the development of transferable skills. These are skills that students can use in most things they do in school and beyond – skills that can be equally useful when studying Mathematics, Languages, Art and Sport, to name but a few. They are skills that students can use even when they are not in school. By now, you know what these skills are. The clue in any Global Perspectives syllabus is in the assessment objectives. These describe what students need to be able to do in order to be successful in the assessment components. The assessment objectives are broken down further depending on the level of study, and the relevant syllabus will help you with this. We have already defined the

Approaches to learning and teaching Global Perspectives

Global Perspectives assessment objectives, but let's remind ourselves here. They are:

- research, evaluation and analysis
- reflection
- communication and collaboration.

As you can see, these assessment objectives refer to skills, not content.

The purpose of the global topics

Depending on the level of study, the global topics identified in the syllabus will help you develop the transferable skills described by the assessment objectives. For example, when developing your students' research skills, you might like to start with the global topic of biodiversity and ecosystem loss. You can then continue to develop students' research skills at a later date using the global topic of the digital world.

While this book gives many suggestions and ideas for activities that you can use with your students to develop these skills, you will want to source some of your own texts and materials that are relevant to the country and context in which you and your students are living and working. This gives you scope for using current, relevant and interesting materials that you and your students can source from a variety of online media.

Some teachers might see this focus on skills as a challenge as they are mostly used to teaching content rather than skills. Look at it as an exciting challenge. Global Perspectives gives you the flexibility to decide on the content of your lessons. This cannot be said about many school subjects. You will find ideas for developing students' skills and resources you can use throughout this book.

Teacher Tip

Due to the transdisciplinary nature of Global Perspectives, its teachers often work closely with other subject teachers to source resources and materials they can use in their lessons. It's also a good idea to know what other subject teachers are teaching so that you can build on the knowledge that students already have. If possible, share ideas or collaborate with colleagues on overlapping themes. For example, you can develop students' speaking skills by holding a debate about whether sustainable living is possible in the 21st century if you know that students have already done quite a lot of work in Geography about sustainable development.

What are my students learning?

The clue for what students are learning is in the title of the subject, Global Perspectives. Students are encouraged to consider issues from different perspectives and viewpoints within these perspectives. Once students have explored different perspectives on an issue by conducting research, they formulate their own personal perspective based on the evidence that they have discovered. Each of your students' personal perspectives will be different, influenced by their cultural background and nationality, as well as by the information they find out during their Global Perspectives studies.

Figure 3.2: Different perspectives.

The different perspectives students consider are global, national, local, personal and cultural, as shown in Figure 3.3. Each of these perspectives can influence each other. The study of Global Perspectives as a subject provides opportunities for enquiry into, and reflection on, key global issues from these different perspectives.

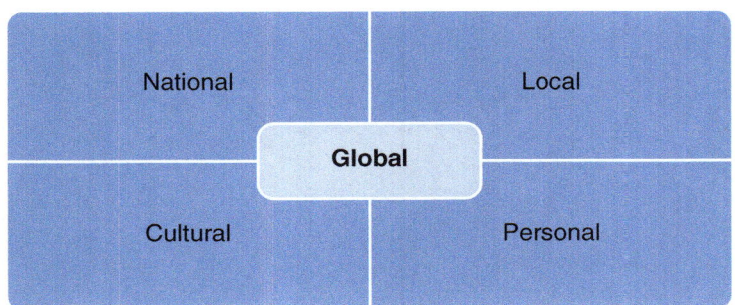

Figure 3.3: How different perspectives influence each other.

Teacher Tip

Some students find it difficult to understand what a perspective is. You can explain that a perspective is a particular way of looking at something. Perspectives are formed by our experiences – by what we have read, heard, learnt and done in our lives. When asking students to consider the global perspective, get them to think about a situation or issue as it relates to the rest of the world, not just to one country (this is a national perspective) or to a community (a local perspective) within a country. They may use case studies to exemplify the global perspective, and should try to use three or four example case studies when giving a global perspective.

As well as considering global issues from different perspectives, students will be applying critical thinking skills to their work, life and directly to the world around them.

Critical thinking skills

When students ask you what critical thinking has to do with Global Perspectives, you can tell them that, as well as reading and listening to texts, they will be questioning what they read and hear to form their own judgements about global issues. They will be using the evidence they gather from research to hold discussions and debates, and produce presentations and video clips to raise awareness of global issues and persuade others of their importance.

Critical thinking in Global Perspectives includes exploring the following ten terms:

1 claim
2 drawing a conclusion
3 statement of argument
4 bias
5 vested interest
6 reasoning
7 evidence
8 problem-solving
9 decision-making
10 empathy.

Teacher Tip

You might like to see how many critical thinking terms your students know. You can give them definitions to see if they can match the correct definition with the correct critical thinking term. They could do this in pairs and then share their answers with another pair to see if they got them all correct.

Here are some example definitions, which avoid using the critical thinking term:

- stating that something is true
- explaining something in a clear, logical and rational way
- having a personal reason for involvement or interest, especially expecting a financial or other gain
- improving or dealing with a difficult or challenging situation
- thinking about and arriving at a conclusion about how to do something
- being for or against one person or a group of people, especially in a way that's considered unfair
- arriving at a judgement or decision based on reasoning
- including facts, opinions, value judgements and predictions
- showing compassion and understanding for the situations of others
- using the available facts or information to support an argument.

Students develop their collaboration and communication skills by working in groups and teams, and they evaluate and reflect on this collaboration and their own contributions to group work. Evaluating sources of information, evidence, reasoning and outcomes is also part of student learning during their Global Perspectives course. You will find plenty of ideas and activities that you can use with your students to develop these skills in the rest of the book.

☑ LESSON IDEA ONLINE 3.3: EXPLORING ISSUES
Use this lesson idea to ask students to explore an issue from different perspectives, as a good group activity to develop collaboration skills.

3

Approaches to learning and teaching Global Perspectives

Key challenges students might face when studying Global Perspectives

One of the main challenges students might face when studying Global Perspectives is to think that they must know everything that there is to know about a topic. They might also worry that their teacher is not actually teaching them, as they are learning in a different way. This can be overcome by explaining to students how the Global Perspectives course differs from other subjects and that Global Perspectives often requires students to reflect on their own, or with other students.

Another concern is that there is a lot of reading and writing, and students might think that their language skills are not good enough to cope with this. You can refer to Chapter 8 **Language awareness** for strategies to help support students with English as a second or third language and Chapter 9 **Inclusive education** for ideas to make Global Perspectives lessons more inclusive.

Teacher Tip

To stop students worrying about there being a lot of reading and writing to do in Global Perspectives, you might tell them that they will be able to choose their own texts and that these can be from podcasts, video clips, cartoons or blogs, and so on. Students will also use images for skill development (there are further ideas for using visuals in Chapter 8 **Language awareness**).

You can suggest that students keep a notebook; then every time they access a resource they should copy and paste the website address into their notebook and make their own notes. One way of encouraging students to take notes is to ask them to identify and write down just five things from a text. You might give clues for the five things such as facts, opinions, value judgements, predictions, issues, perspectives, causes, consequences, courses of action, and so on.

Alternatively, you might let students decide on the most important five things and then ask them to share with a partner to see if the partner has the same. Pairs should then explain to each other why they chose those five things.

How is my students' learning being assessed?

Just as lessons for Global Perspectives are driven by skills rather than content, so is the summative assessment. Students are expected to demonstrate that they can:

- research, analyse and evaluate sources of information and evidence
- develop and justify an argument made up of different lines of reasoning
- reflect on their own work and learning
- communicate information, arguments and perspectives
- collaborate to achieve a common goal.

Depending on their level of study, students' learning is assessed summatively by writing a research report, by collaborating on a team project and by completing a written examination that uses source material as the content for addressing the questions asked. These are all explored further in other chapters of this book, including Chapter 5 **Active learning**, Chapter 6 **Assessment for Learning** and Chapter 11 **Global thinking**.

☑ LESSON IDEA ONLINE 3.4: GLOBAL PERSPECTIVES QUIZ

Use this lesson idea as an Assessment for Learning quiz to see how much students already know about Global Perspectives. You can ask students to mark each other's work and give feedback on their answers. Further Assessment for Learning ideas are considered in Chapter 6 **Assessment for Learning**.

Key challenges students might face when being assessed in Global Perspectives

The main challenge for students when being assessed in Global Perspectives is being confident about their ability to do what the assessment tasks require. For coursework tasks, we have already noted that students can get disheartened if there is a lot of reading and writing. Some students also think that when they find a good article or website they cannot phrase the content any better, and so make the mistake of copying and pasting. Encouraging students to build up notes in their notebooks will increase their confidence to write their own research reports and team projects.

For a written examination, students can feel that they are not prepared. The main reason for this is that it's difficult to revise for a Global

Perspectives written examination in the same way that they would for other subjects, as it does not assess content. Instead it assesses skills, notably those of analysis and evaluation.

▣ LESSON IDEA ONLINE 3.5: COMPARING WRITTEN RESPONSES

Use this lesson idea as a way of building students' confidence for the Global Perspectives written examination.

Teacher Tip

Use past examination papers to prepare your students for the Global Perspectives written examination. You don't have to use whole papers; you can choose questions that students feel less confident about. Often, these are the questions that attract the most marks and demand higher order thinking skills, like analysis and evaluation.

As well as asking students to complete individual questions for teacher, peer or self-assessment, you can use exemplar answers for students to compare. You can often get these from training events or on the support website for the qualification. You might even use exemplars of answers written by students from previous years.

Summary

This chapter has focused on the nature of Global Perspectives as a subject and the key things you might need to consider when delivering a Global Perspectives course. Look back over the material to ensure your understanding of the following:

- Global Perspectives emphasises the development of skills, not the teaching of content.

- Regardless of the level of study, the Global Perspectives assessment objectives (skills) are research, analysis, evaluation, reflection, communication and collaboration.

- The lessons you design will use global topics to develop students' skills, but students are not required to know all there is about a global topic.

Interpreting a syllabus

4

Working with a syllabus document

Having made the decision to start teaching Global Perspectives, the next stage is to study the syllabus that you want to teach in detail. All qualifications have a syllabus document, and Global Perspectives is no exception. The syllabus document is your starting point. It will give you all the key information you need to start building your course for your own students and context.

Teacher Tip

Syllabus documents are accessible on an examination body's website. Use your search engine and type in the syllabus you want and the year that your students will be sitting the examination. This way you'll know that you have the correct syllabus. The last thing you want is to be telling your students the wrong thing. Remember that there is often more than one syllabus for a subject so it's a good idea to know the number/code of the syllabus you want.

The purpose of a syllabus

A syllabus is a short guide to the subject. Its purpose is to provide essential information only. An examining body cannot know the range of teachers that will teach a syllabus they design or the range of students that will sit the summative assessment tasks at the end of the course. It can only ensure that no matter where a student or teacher is in the world, they all have the same syllabus and the same information for the same subject at that level. By providing a syllabus, examining bodies also know that teachers and students are getting the same information about the requirements for the summative assessment tasks for that qualification.

☑ **LESSON IDEA ONLINE 4.1: CREATING A 'CAN DO' LIST**
Use this lesson idea to introduce your chosen Global Perspectives syllabus to your students.

Having a long-term plan

Once you have read and understood the syllabus, you need to produce a long-term plan of what you want your students to learn throughout their Global Perspectives course. The syllabus determines some of this. That is, the skills as assessment objectives are defined, as you explored using Lesson idea 4.1.

Your long-term plan should culminate in the summative assessment tasks. It is a bit like a road map that guides you and your Global Perspectives students to the final destination. When they reach their destination, students should be equipped and able to complete the required summative assessment tasks.

The three key questions to think about before you start to teach your Global Perspectives course are:

- How much time do I need?
- Which skills do I need to develop?
- Which topics shall I use?

How much time do I need?

Each syllabus sets out recommended guided learning hours. For example, Cambridge IGCSE qualifications recommend 130 guided learning hours, which equates to about two hours per week over two years or four hours per week over one year, depending on your school year. This does not include any independent work that students do at school or at home. Guided learning time is time when they are actively engaged in learning and you are facilitating this, either by delivering an activity to develop a specific skill or by monitoring and giving feedback as students take part in a learning activity. Global Perspectives requires the same amount of time as any other subject. Skills take time to develop. Think about how long it took you to learn to drive or to become good at a sport. You might still be learning …

Which skills do I need to develop?

We know which skills Global Perspectives requires students to show competence in, but do you know how well developed these skills already are in the students you will be teaching? If you find out, you might be able to spend longer on the specific skills students are less competent in. You are lucky if you are starting to teach a class that has already studied Global Perspectives before they get to you or has had teachers that have concentrated on skills development as well as teaching content, for example in English Language or Social Science classes.

> ☑ **LESSON IDEA ONLINE 4.2: SKILLS ASSESSMENT**
>
> Use this lesson idea as a self-assessment activity to get students to consider how well their skills are developed. You can ask them to do the activity at the start of their Global Perspectives course and then return to it at regular intervals to see if there has been progress. There are further Assessment for Learning ideas in Chapter 6 **Assessment for Learning**.

Which topics shall we use?

In the section entitled, 'Using global topics and issues within these topics', in Chapter 5 **Active learning**, there is one idea for how you might choose the global topics for developing students' skills. You could also ask students to complete a diamond nine activity, as in Lesson idea 4.3.

> ☑ **LESSON IDEA ONLINE 4.3: DIAMOND NINE**
>
> Use this lesson idea to get students to identify and prioritise the global topics the class is interested in.

Putting together your long-term plan

If you have tried out the lesson ideas in this chapter, your students know the assessment objectives. You also know where they think their strengths lie and the areas they feel need developing. You will also know this from their previous teachers and if you have taught the students before. Your students have also made you aware of the topics they are interested in. You are now ready to put together your long-term plan.

Your long-term plan sets out what you want students to learn over the course of study. It might look something like Table 4.1, depending on the global topics within which you have chosen to develop the skills. This long-term plan is based on three terms per year (two lessons per week plus independent learning) over two years. Notice that this long-term plan places more emphasis on the skills of evaluation, reflection and communication (appearing three times) as this teacher felt that these were the weakest skills of their students. However, the other skills have not been ignored and all appear twice in this plan. Your plan will probably look different from this one for the reasons mentioned previously. Remember, you don't have to 'teach' all the global topics. You don't even need as many as this; you might prefer to focus on just two global topics per term to develop your students' skills.

Term 1	Term 2	Term 3	Term 4	Term 5	Term 6
Research: tradition, culture, identity	Communication: digital world	*Produce first coursework*	Evaluation: humans and other species	Analysis: education for all	Evaluation: migration
Analysis: sustainability	Collaboration: disease and health	Communication: language and communication	Reflection: conflict and peace	Research: demographic change	Communication: fuel and energy
Evaluation: family	Reflection: poverty and inequality	Collaboration: human rights	*Produce second coursework*	Reflection: fuel and energy	*Practise for written examination*

Table 4.1: An example of a Global Perspectives teaching plan.

Using the syllabus to design a programme of learning

Now that you have a long-term plan, you can focus on your programme of learning. A programme of learning is another term for a scheme of work or a mid-term plan. The rest of this book will explore how you might put together a programme of learning for Global Perspectives in your school. Other chapters give you further ideas to consider when creating your Global Perspectives course. For example, Chapter 5 **Active learning** gives plenty of ideas for activities to develop students' skills, and Chapter 6 **Assessment for Learning** focuses on Assessment for Learning strategies to help you monitor the progress and achievements of your students.

4 Approaches to learning and teaching Global Perspectives

The top ten things to include in a programme of learning and chapter references for further guidance are:

1 skill focus (Chapters 4, 5, 6 and 9)
2 global topic (Chapters 4, 5 and 11)
3 learning outcome (Chapters 5 and 9)
4 learning objective(s) (Chapters 5 and 9)
5 success criteria (Chapter 6)
6 teaching and learning activities (all chapters)
7 opportunities for support and stretch to enable inclusive education (Chapter 9)
8 timing (e.g. ten hours)
9 materials and resources (Chapters 5, 6, 7, 8, 9, 10 and 11)
10 Assessment for Learning (Chapter 6).

Producing a programme of learning for Global Perspectives doesn't have to be left up to you, as the teacher. Students can and should be involved in the design of their programme of learning.

☑ LESSON IDEA ONLINE 4.4: MEDIUM-TERM PLANNING

Use this lesson idea as a starting point for designing a Global Perspectives programme of learning. You can use and adapt this idea at the start of any new topic.

Summary

In this chapter, we have explored how to interpret a syllabus so that you have a long-term and medium-term plan to design lessons from.

Remember the following:

- The syllabus sets out the skills as assessment objectives and requirements for the summative assessment tasks.

- You can choose which global topics you use from the syllabus to develop your students' skills.

- Your students can help with your long-term and medium-term planning.

Active learning

5

What is active learning?

Active learning is a pedagogical practice that places student learning at its centre. It focuses on *how* students learn, not just on *what* they learn. We as teachers need to encourage students to 'think hard', rather than passively receive information. Active learning encourages students to take responsibility for their learning and supports them in becoming independent and confident learners in school and beyond.

Research shows us that it is not possible to transmit understanding to students by simply telling them what they need to know. Instead, we need to make sure that we challenge students' thinking and support them in building their own understanding. Active learning encourages more complex thought processes, such as evaluating, analysing and synthesising, which foster a greater number of neural connections in the brain. While some students may be able to create their own meaning from information received passively, others will not. Active learning enables all students to build knowledge and understanding in response to the opportunities we provide.

Why adopt an active learning approach?

We can enrich all areas of the curriculum, at all stages, by embedding an active learning approach.

In active learning, we need to think not only about the content but also about the process. It gives students greater involvement and control over their learning. This encourages all students to stay focused on their learning, which will often give them greater enthusiasm for their studies. Active learning is intellectually stimulating, and taking this approach encourages a level of academic discussion with our students that we, as teachers, can also enjoy. Healthy discussion means that students are engaging with us as a partner in their learning.

Students will better be able to revise for examinations in the sense that revision really is 're-vision' of the ideas that they already understand.

Active learning develops students' analytical skills, supporting them to be better problem solvers and more effective in their application of knowledge. They will be prepared to deal with challenging and unexpected situations. As a result, students are more confident in continuing to learn once they have left school and are better equipped for the transition to higher education and the workplace.

What are the challenges of incorporating active learning?

When people start thinking about putting active learning into practice, they often make the mistake of thinking more about the activity they want to design than about the learning. The most important thing is to put the student and the learning at the centre of our planning. A task can be quite simple but still get the student to think critically and independently. Sometimes a complicated task does not actually help to develop the students' thinking or understanding at all. We need to consider carefully what we want our students to learn or understand and then shape the task to activate this learning.

Planning for student-centred learning

Once you have your designed your programme of study from the syllabus (see Chapter 4 **Interpreting a syllabus**), you need to design appropriate sequences of learning to enable the development of the skills discussed in Chapter 3 **The nature of the subject and key considerations**.

Planning for active learning means planning for student-centred rather than teacher-led learning. We know that students develop their understanding through language, so it's important that you give students opportunities to read, listen, write and discuss. The study of Global Perspectives offers many opportunities for student-centred learning. Global Perspectives does not require students to remember all there is to know about a global topic. Students research and consider different perspectives on an issue. They question these perspectives, and the information and sources of evidence they find. They then draw their own conclusions based on this evidence. This is active learning in Global Perspectives. By definition, active learning makes students more independent in their learning – relying less and less on the teacher. Before reading on, consider the extent to which you think your Global Perspectives lessons promote active learning and what you might be able to do to make your lessons more student-centred.

Creating independent learners does not mean that the teacher has no input. Students will not be able to develop the necessary skills on their own, certainly not at the start of their Global Perspectives learning journey. They need you to design stimulating learning experiences, and they need to receive guidance and feedback on their progress. There is more about this in Chapter 6 **Assessment for Learning**. Some students need more guidance and support (scaffolding) than others, and this is something you will need to plan for. Further guidance about how to have an inclusive classroom is considered in Chapter 9 **Inclusive education**. One way of providing support is to design pair and small group activities so that students can support each other.

Teacher Tip

Think about a class you teach. List all the ways in which you enable students to become more independent; for example, by directing them to use a dictionary for unknown vocabulary, or by teaching them how to do research.

☑ LESSON IDEA ONLINE 5.1: GET ONE – GIVE ONE

Use any global topic in this lesson idea as a good way of getting students to work collaboratively and support each other.

Many of the key ideas about active learning are also key to studying Global Perspectives as a subject. These key ideas about active learning state that new learning:

• is built on previous knowledge and understanding
• should be relevant and happen within a meaningful context
• is developmental
• involves students as participants in learning rather than observers.

What each of these means in relation to your Global Perspectives lessons is demonstrated in Figure 5.1 and is the focus of the next section of this chapter.

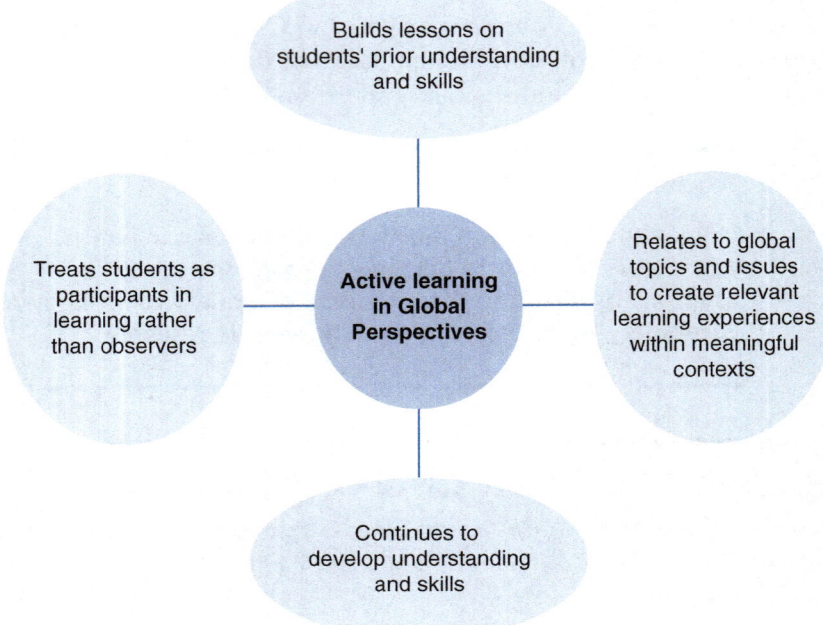

Figure 5.1: Relating active learning to Global Perspectives.

Building on students' prior knowledge and understanding

Global Perspectives promotes active learning in that lessons build on students' prior knowledge and understanding. This might be from their:

- study of other curriculum subjects
- understanding of what is happening in the world around them
- skill level, previously developed either by you or by other teachers.

The first step in providing an environment conducive to active learning is to be clear about what your learning objective for the lesson is. For example, if the lesson objective is 'to be able to distinguish between an opinion, a fact and a prediction and explain how they differ', then the activity at the start of the lesson should try to find out how much understanding students already have about facts, opinions and predictions.

LESSON IDEA 5.2: FACTS, OPINIONS OR PREDICTIONS?

A good starter activity to determine students' understanding of facts, opinions and predictions is to have a series of statements of argument on the board related to one of the global topics or to different global topics (e.g. facts, predictions, opin ons and value judgements). You can then ask students to work in pairs to put these into the different categories. Pairs can then share their ideas with each other, and whole class feedback can establish how much understanding students have before the main activity of the lesson begins.

Teacher Tip

Try to write your learning objective in terms of what you want your students to know, understand or be able to do by the end of the lesson. If you have just one lesson objective, you will find it easier to elicit from students what the success criteria might be.

Here's an example.

Learning objective: Students will be able to evaluate evidence from different sources of information.

Success criteria: Identify and explain strengths and weaknesses of different types of evidence about the causes and consequences of youth unemployment.

You will be exploring success criteria further in Chapter 6 **Assessment for Learning**.

Starter activities

Starter activities are an excellent way of gaining information about what your students already know, understand and are able to do. It is beyond the scope of this book to list all the possible activities that you could use, but we will explore a few ideas that I have tried over the years and that worked well with my students.

Graphic organisers

If you have never used a graphic organiser before, now's the time to start. Graphic organisers help students to organise their ideas and thoughts, often in a visual way using tables and diagrams. One example of a graphic organiser is a KWL (know – want to know – learnt) chart. KWL charts are useful at the start of a lesson to activate and consolidate what has already been learned, but can also be used as an Assessment for Learning strategy in the middle of a lesson as students monitor their learning and progress. Chapter 6 **Assessment for Learning** gives you more ideas for how to monitor the progress and learning of your students.

When using a KWL chart, the most important principle is that students can reflect on what they know (K) and what they want to learn (W), which could include revision of partially forgotten material. Later, either as the lesson progresses or at the end of the lesson by way of a plenary, they record what they have learnt (L). Completing the L column consolidates the new knowledge and understanding, and evidences progress. Some groups benefit from including an additional 'F' column for Finding further information and an 'H' column for How to find this information.

☑ LESSON IDEA ONLINE 5.3: KWL CHART

Use this lesson idea to revise and consolidate students' thoughts and learning about the global topic belief systems.

Teacher Tip

Using questions related to a global topic really focuses students on the issues and the different perspectives. If they do their KWL chart on a Word document on their computer, they can edit their chart by removing notes from the W (want to learn) column and adding notes to the L (have learnt) and K (already know) columns. By doing this, they are really thinking about their own learning and progress.

You need to think of activities that allow students not only to build on what they already know, perhaps from other curriculum subjects, but also to develop their skills. One of these is communication skills. In my experience, students find it easier to talk than to listen. Do you also find this? If the answer is yes, then developing students' listening skills should be included in your Global Perspectives programme plan/scheme of work.

Figure 5.2: Students taking turns to listen to each other.

☑ LESSON IDEA ONLINE 5.4: LISTENING ACTIVITY
Use this lesson idea as a way of developing your students' listening skills.

Don't forget that all lesson ideas in this book can be adapted to suit your students and the global topic(s) they are interested in as a way of developing their skills. That's the beauty of Global Perspectives, in that the content is not prescribed. You can use global topics that are of interest to you and your students. As a linguist, I choose to develop my students' skills by exploring the topics of tradition, culture and identity, changing communities, and language and communication. I have built up a bank of resources (listening and reading texts and suitable websites) for these topics. I then allow my students to choose a couple of other topics for developing their skills. These change depending on the group of students. Recent, popular choices include globalisation, education for all and the digital world.

Using global topics to create relevant learning experiences

The principle for using global topics and issues within these topics is that we learn best when we can see the usefulness of what we learn and connect it to the real world. What could be more relevant and meaningful a context for new learning than considering issues that are happening not only globally, but also nationally and locally, and that affect students personally? This is the aim of Global Perspectives – to explore issues from global, national, local and personal perspectives and viewpoints within these perspectives: viewpoints such as those of scientists, politicians, economists, and so on.

Teacher Tip

Consider narrowing down the list of global topics that you plan to use to develop skills to five or six topics over the length of the programme. This will prevent you from falling into the trap of teaching every topic and all about every topic. Try to narrow the list to ten topics to start with, including your favourites and topics you know will have resources, especially for the national perspective. Then give students a choice. You can do this by asking them to work in pairs to put the topics in order, with 1 being their favourite and 10 being their least favourite. You can then collect their choices and tell them what the most popular five or six were. In this way, your students will feel that they have contributed to lesson planning and they are less likely to find fault with the topics chosen. You also know what your students are interested in, so you can plan lessons to meet their interests as well as their needs.

Some global topics lend themselves more to team projects than others. This is because they can be broken down into issues that teams can raise awareness about, showing different cultural perspectives. Good examples include poverty and inequality, disease and health, and tradition, culture and identity. For example, an aim for a project might be to raise awareness about the different cultural perspectives on homelessness.

Some global topics, on the other hand, lend themselves more to individual research and a written report based on this research: for example, humans and other species, sustainable living, and biodiversity and ecosystem loss. A question that could be asked, for example, is 'Are humans responsible for ecosystem loss?' Rather than showing different cultural perspectives, these topics are useful for exploring issues from global, national and local perspectives, and proposing courses of action to help resolve or improve the identified issues.

It doesn't matter which global topics and issues you use to develop your students' skills in your Global Perspectives lessons. You will, however, need to check your syllabus to clarify any requirements for specific topics for different summative assessment tasks.

☑ LESSON IDEA ONLINE 5.5: USING VIDEO CLIPS
Use this lesson idea to encourage students to source their own information about a global topic and issues within that topic.

Global topics and issues within these play an important role when asking students to explore different perspectives. Sometimes students struggle to consider an issue from different perspectives and they just give information about a country. It's important that students understand that the national perspective relates to the view of the country where the student lives. For example, the global perspective might be that water is scarce and we need to use it sparingly as otherwise we'll run out. In a country where it rains a lot and there is an abundance of rivers and lakes, the national perspective might be very different.

Teacher Tip

To prevent students from simply giving information about a country, encourage them to use the following words and phrases in their work: believes, thinks, is of the opinion, perspective is, view is, according to …, as far as … is concerned, take the viewpoint that, the position of … is, and so on.

When looking at perspectives, students should understand that people see the world differently because their experiences and ways of thinking differ. Indeed, as your students work through their Global Perspectives course, they might alter their perspective according to what they find out and experience.

> ⊡ **LESSON IDEA ONLINE 5.6: DIFFERENT PERSPECTIVES**
> Use this lesson idea to get students to reflect on their personal perspective about an issue before and after taking part in a debate.

Learning is developmental

Global Perspectives is a developmental course of study which has the potential to move students from developing through to established and enhanced skills so that they become more proficient with practice.

When analysing issues, students will need more scaffolding at the start of their Global Perspectives course. Indeed, as analysis is one of the Global Perspectives assessment objectives, it will be summatively assessed at various stages of your students' Global Perspectives learning journey. You need to ensure that their skills of analysis are well developed. Refer back to Chapter 3 **The nature of the subject and key considerations** to read more about this.

Figure 5.3: Scaffolding learning.

> **☑ LESSON IDEA ONLINE 5.7: SCAFFOLDING LEARNING - ANALYSIS**
> Use this lesson idea as a way of scaffolding your students' learning as they develop their skills of analysis.

Scaffolding learning ensures that all students can participate in learning and are appropriately challenged. We will explore ideas for making your lessons inclusive further in Chapter 9 **Inclusive education**.

Teacher Tip

Advise students that when they are looking for causes, they should look for words like: because, since, due to, as.

When looking for consequences, they should look for words like: as a result, therefore, thus, that's why, so.

They can also use these words in their own writing when talking about the causes and consequences of issues.

Students as participants in learning rather than observers

As teachers, we want students to be well motivated and active participants in lessons. You may already be aware that there are four common reasons why students don't participate:

1 They are learning the same things over and over again. This might happen in Global Perspectives if we mistakenly teach content rather than develop skills. For example, if we teach about global warming, our students might get bored as they have already done this topic in other subjects. They will be more motivated if we develop their communication skills and give them the opportunity to demonstrate what they know by holding a debate about whether global warming can be slowed down or stopped.

LESSON IDEA 5.8: PRACTISING SKILLS

Divide your class into groups depending on the skills they need to practise so that they can really focus on what they need help with. You can choose any text and use it for all the groups.

- Ask one group to summarise the text in no more than 100 words.
- One group identifies issues and perspectives.
- Another group looks for statements of argument (facts, opinions, predictions and value judgements).
- A fourth group produces something to raise awareness about the issue (a poem, song, poster, and so on).
- The last group writes some questions that can be answered using the text.

You can move between the groups to monitor progress.

2   What they are learning is too hard. As discussed earlier in this chapter, learning is developmental, so if the material is too hard it can lower interest and motivation. We need to scaffold learning, including adapting texts so that they are appropriately challenging and age appropriate.

LESSON IDEA 5.9: THE JIGSAW METHOD

If you haven't already done so, give the jigsaw method a try. Choose a suitable text and cut it up into five pieces. Divide your class into five groups and ask each group to read and discuss one of the text pieces. For example, one group might be reading about the reasons for migration. Another might be reading about the consequences, and so on. These groups become the class 'experts' on their piece of text. Then split the class into five new groups that include one 'expert' on each piece of text. Ask these new groups to work together to produce a presentation or a podcast that requires information from the whole text. As the group works together, they will be teaching each other and producing something creative.

3   They are simply reading or listening to information. As long ago as 1946, Edgar Dale, an American educationalist, discovered that after

two weeks, we remember only about 20% of what we hear, whereas we tend to remember 90% of what we say and do.

LESSON IDEA 5.10: PEER ASSESSMENT

It's a good idea to give students something to do when listening to you or other students. Asking students to peer assess and give feedback is an excellent way of enabling them to connect to what they are hearing and seeing.

4   The lessons are teacher–led rather than student–centred. In student-centred lessons, students do 80% of the work and the teacher does 20%. Ask yourself whether you only do 20% of the work in your Global Perspectives lessons.

Summary

In this chapter, we have explored how active learning involves students as participants in learning during Global Perspectives lessons.

Remember the following when designing learning for your Global Perspectives students:

- Active learning promotes student-centred rather than teacher-led learning.

- Active learning builds on students' prior knowledge, understanding and skills.

- Learning is developmental, and the development of skills takes time and needs scaffolding.

6 | Assessment for Learning

What is Assessment for Learning?

Assessment for Learning (AfL) is a teaching approach that generates feedback that can be used to improve students' performance. Students become more involved in the learning process and, from this, gain confidence in what they are expected to learn and to what standard. We as teachers gain insights into a student's level of understanding of a particular concept or topic, which helps to inform how we support their progression.

We need to understand the meaning and method of giving purposeful feedback to optimise learning. Feedback can be informal, such as oral comments to help students think through problems, or formal, such as through the use of rubrics to help clarify and scaffold learning and assessment objectives.

Why use Assessment for Learning?

By following well-designed approaches to AfL, we can understand better how our students are learning and use this to plan what we will do next with a class or individual students (see Figure 6.1). We can help our students to see what they are aiming for and to understand what they need to do to get there. AfL makes learning visible; it helps students understand more accurately the nature of the material they are learning and themselves as learners. The quality of interactions and feedback between students and teachers becomes critical to the learning process.

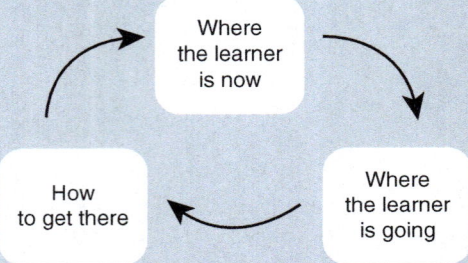

Figure 6.1: How can we use this plan to help our students?

We can use AfL to help our students focus on specific elements of their learning and to take greater responsibility for how they might move forward. AfL creates a valuable connection between assessment and learning activities, as the clarification of objectives will have a direct impact on how we devise teaching and learning strategies. AfL techniques can support students in becoming more confident in what they are learning, reflective in how they are learning, more likely to try out new approaches, and more engaged in what they are being asked to learn.

What are the challenges of incorporating AfL?

The use of AfL does not mean that we need to test students more frequently. It would be easy to just increase the amount of summative assessment and use this formatively as a regular method of helping us decide what to do next in our teaching. We can judge how much learning has taken place through ways other than testing, including, above all, communicating with our students in a variety of ways and getting to know them better as individuals.

Assessment for Learning to develop skills

You are probably already familiar with some AfL strategies, as you might have previously taught a more content-based course like Geography or History. However, you may be finding it a challenge designing assessment tasks that assess the development of skills, which is what teaching Global Perspectives asks you to do, as opposed to testing content. As we discovered in Chapter 4 **Interpreting a syllabus**, the only content in Global Perspectives is the topics and issues you choose to explore to develop your students' skills, so there is no need for you to test content. This is a liberating thought, but it presents its own challenges, which this chapter will help you with.

Teacher Tip

You probably do this already, but you can do more of it in Global Perspectives lessons as students direct much of their own learning. When students are working in pairs and in small groups, wander around the room, listening to conversations and observing how students are interacting with each other. When they are working independently, or with others, ask questions to check understanding and provide the necessary guidance and support. By doing these things, you can get immediate feedback about whether students are meeting the learning objective(s) you have set.

Assessment for Learning as standard practice for skills development

As Global Perspectives teachers, we could fall into the trap of being mostly concerned with our own performance in the classroom, the information we know, and what and how we are going to teach it. The students and their learning then become secondary – this happened to me a lot when I first started teaching. However, if we realise that our role is more about guiding the learning, enabling our students to do more for themselves in terms of the skills required – research, analysis, evaluation, reflection, communication and collaboration – we also realise the importance of AfL. It's important, not only for students to know where they are and where they're going, but also for us as teachers to help them reach that next step.

As Figure 6.2 shows, where your students start depends on the step they are aiming towards. They might be new to skill development and start on the first step. Once they have gained some understanding, they move to the next step, at established skill level. When they master the skill at a higher level, they will be on the top step (enhanced skill level) and you can now rely on them to perhaps help others. You will only know what step students are on if you regularly use AfL strategies.

Figure 6.2: Assessment for Learning to reach the next step.

> **☑ LESSON IDEA ONLINE 6.1: TEACHING PAIRS**
> Use this lesson idea to help you assess your students' understanding of how to find relevant information. You can determine the pairs beforehand. This lesson idea will also work with small groups of three.

Assessing different skills

Hopefully, you found Lesson idea 6.1 a useful way of assessing your students' skills in terms of being able to find relevant information. With this evidence, you can now plan how you are going to develop this skill further. As you will have seen, asking students to teach each other is a great way of not only establishing and enhancing their own skill level, but also enabling them to peer- and self-assess. Both are excellent forms of AfL. We will now focus on how you might assess the development of students' skills for Global Perspective, which includes information skills under the umbrella of the skill of 'research'.

Teacher Tip

Rather than pairing different students every lesson, you may want to consider having student 'learning buddies' in lessons, where the same students 'buddy' each other for a period of time, sharing ideas and guiding and supporting each other when necessary. By doing this, you can circulate around the classroom more, and you give students more responsibility for their own learning. You can change the learning buddies every six weeks or so to enable students to work with others, explaining that students will gain different ideas and perspectives from different learning buddies.

Figure 6.3: Learning buddies.

Assessing the development of research skills

Research skills play an important role in Global Perspectives, as the topics and issues students use to develop the other skills (analysis, evaluation, reflection, communication and collaboration) focus on what's going on in the world around us today. The only way of doing this is by some form of research, which can be done by you as the teacher and by your students. By developing your students' research skills, not only are you empowering them, but you will also ultimately have less work to do as students will become more able to find their own information and rely less on your research ability to provide relevant texts.

☑ LESSON IDEA ONLINE 6.2: PRE-ASSESSING RESEARCH SKILLS

Use this lesson idea to pre-assess your students' research skills. This could be done when you first meet your Global Perspectives class and you know little about what they have been doing in terms of research beforehand. You can choose the amount and range of questions you ask depending on the age and ability of the group of students. The worksheet can be adapted to suit your needs.

The skill of research can be broken down further into different areas, such as constructing research questions, developing information skills, conducting research and recording findings. You might want to use the questionnaire in the Lesson idea 6.2 worksheet to assess progress in all of these or you might decide on a different way of assessing your students' progress, such as Lesson idea 6.1 for assessing information skills.

Teacher Tip

When doing any research on the internet, always advise students to copy and paste the website address they get information from into a Word document and add the title of the article, the date, the author and the date accessed. In this way, they can keep track of the sources of information they use for a particular purpose. It also encourages good study skills (particularly if they are going on to further study at university, for example).

Example: Laycock, K. (2016) *Assessing Research Skills*. Online: www.greatarticleaboutassessmentforlearning.com (accessed 16/07/2016).

Assessing the development of the skills of analysis and evaluation

Although they are not the same skill, we have grouped analysis and evaluation together here as they both demand higher order thinking skills, which are often difficult skills for students to develop and equally challenging for teachers to assess. These higher order thinking skills ask more of students than to simply describe, which is often what many students do. Sometimes, however, we make the mistake of assuming that students know how to analyse and evaluate, and very often they do not, so it's up to us to develop these skills. One way of looking at the role of AfL is to 'close the gap' between where a student is at the moment and where you and they want them to be.

Teacher Tip

There are many assessment strategies, including those we have seen – peer feedback and self-assessment using a questionnaire. Others include 'traffic lights' where students hold up red for lack of understanding or ability, amber for some understanding or ability and green for full understanding or ability.

What's important to note, however, is that the AfL strategy is only beneficial if it gives you the information you need to close the learning gap and move your students forwards. As well as the age of your students, the AfL strategy you use depends on the skill you are trying to assess.

While assessment strategies such as 'traffic lights' might give you the information you need to assess whether your students understand the difference between a fact, an opinion, a value judgement, a prediction or bias, or deciding whether they feel that they have achieved a learning objective, it is unlikely that they will give you information about the development of your students' skills of analysis and evaluation. You will need to use different strategies to assess this. Lesson idea 6.3 gives you a suggestion.

☑ LESSON IDEA ONLINE 6.3: ASSESSING ANALYSIS

Use this lesson idea to determine students' skills in terms of developing analysis and evaluation. You can use any text from any of the Global Perspectives topics. Once you know their skills level and where you want them to get to, you can plan how to close that gap.

When assessing your students' ability to analyse an issue in Global Perspectives, you will want to see that they first understand what the issue is, and then they will need to be able to identify and explain the causes and consequences of the issue. It is not enough that they simply identify the issue as this demands a lower level of thinking than explaining. By explaining, they are in fact analysing.

When evaluating sources, you need to advise students to consider the strengths and weaknesses of the source of information and explain why they think these are strengths and weaknesses. For example, weaknesses might include that the information is biased, that it does not support the claim made, or that it is considered unreliable. Strengths could be that the source quotes experts in the field to support the claims made, that it is up to date and that the information provided can be cross–referenced as accurate.

Assessing students' ability to reflect

Global Perspectives asks students to be reflective. As we discovered in Chapter 5 **Active learning**, there are many ways in which you can encourage your students to be more reflective about their learning. For AfL purposes, being able to reflect means being able to answer the questions 'how?' and 'why?' in relation to learning so that you can determine 'what' needs to be done next, as shown in Figure 6.4.

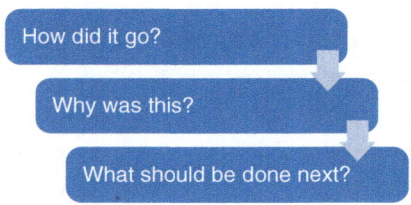

Figure 6.4: Effective reflection.

Teacher Tip

The best way of guiding your students to become more reflective is by being a reflective practitioner yourself. Don't be afraid to model reflective practice in your lessons. For example, at the start of a lesson, you might say something like, 'I've been looking again at our last lesson. From your feedback, it seems that some of you are still a bit confused about the difference between analysis and evaluation, and want some more examples. I've thought about it and I have an activity for you to do to clarify the difference.'

As you are focusing on discovering the extent to which your students can reflect, you need to design AfL tasks that allow them to do so. As well as using the lesson ideas for reflection in Chapter 5 **Active learning** as quick, short AfL tasks, you can also use pieces of writing that students might actually do for their Global Perspectives summative assessment tasks.

☑ LESSON IDEA ONLINE 6.4: SUMMATIVE ASSESSMENT AS ASSESSMENT FOR LEARNING

This is a summative assessment task, to be used only in a formative assessment (AfL) way. Students assess a piece of reflective writing using assessment criteria. As a follow-up, students do a practice piece of reflective writing and assess each other's against the assessment criteria. This means that, although students might have to do this as part of their examination, they are doing a practice piece and can therefore gain some feedback. When they come to do a final reflective piece, their reflective skills should have improved.

You will see that the piece of reflective writing is assessed using assessment criteria. Each student's piece of reflective writing should also be written using the same assessment criteria.

Using success criteria to assess students' ability to communicate

As well as using assessment criteria, you can use success criteria to establish where students are in their learning. These success criteria should come from the learning objective set for the lesson. For example, if the learning objective is 'Participate in discussion tasks, showing understanding of active listening skills', the success criteria might be 'Students show active listening skills in pair work to discuss and agree on answers to questions about the effects of globalisation.' If the aim is to write a balanced argument, then your success criteria might look something like this:

Learning objective: To write a balanced argument

Success criteria: I must …

- write in the third person
- use links and signposts to structure work
- use statements of argument, for example facts, predictions
- write four paragraphs.

Paragraph 1 – Introduce the argument.

Paragraph 2 – The argument from one perspective.

Paragraph 3 – The argument from another perspective.

Paragraph 4 – Conclusion: the most reasonable argument that gives my opinion.

Teacher Tip

Learning objectives are useful to guide the direction of the learning, but often these are too vague for students to recognise how to be successful in achieving them, particularly for Global Perspectives where, as you know, the focus is on skills. So using specific success criteria can help. You can even share the learning objectives with students and ask them to come up with success criteria. This is effective AfL.

Questioning in Global Perspectives lessons

One way to actively involve your students in their own learning is by using questions. Effective questioning is a great AfL strategy. That's not to say that you have to ask all the questions. Global Perspectives encourages students to ask questions too.

Teacher Tip

You may want to try questioning using mini whiteboards. They are a great way for getting answers from individual students. All students need is a mini whiteboard or laminated piece of white A4 card, a black dry-wipe pen and an eraser (piece of cloth or tissue). You can set a question that has three marks, for example, 'Identify a fact from this text and explain why you think it's a fact', and wander around the room with your non-black dry-wipe pen, ticking correct points and/or adding comments such as, 'One more point needed' or 'Check this'.

Assessing students' ability to collaborate

Collaboration is an important Global Perspectives skill and you should look for opportunities to enable your students to develop their collaboration skills. Working together as pairs and small groups on collaborative activities in class will develop collaboration skills, as will more specific team projects. You shouldn't just leave the team project until summative assessment. Students can work together on a team project in preparation for summative assessment. These 'practice' team projects will allow you to see who works well together and allow students to practise the required skills before they do their summative assessment.

Many teachers try to use Bloom's Revised Taxonomy to help them ask better questions. Table 6.1 might give you some ideas for how you can apply it to the questions you ask students in your Global Perspectives lessons.

Level of Bloom's Revised Taxonomy	Five key words	Three example Global Perspectives questions
Remembering	identify, list, select, name, state	Can you identify a fact? What is the issue? Who is it an issue for?
Understanding	explain, compare, summarise, predict, describe	What do you think can be done to improve the situation? Who do think might be affected by the issue? What do you think the causes of the issue are, and why?
Applying	solve, interpret, show, choose, develop	How might you solve this problem? Which argument do you think is better and why? What does the graph in the text show us?

→

Level of Bloom's Revised Taxonomy	Five key words	Three example Global Perspectives questions
Analysing	conclude, analyse, contrast, prioritise, infer	What assumptions does the author make? What conclusions can you draw? Which of the following would you prioritise, and why?
Evaluating	evaluate, assess, judge, justify, support	What are the strengths and weaknesses of the source? What justifications are there for the conclusion given? Which evidence supports the author's perspective?
Creating	test, adapt, imagine, create, propose	How might you test this claim? What changes would you make to improve the situation, and why? Does the outcome you have created meet the proposed project aim?

Table 6.1: Bloom's Revised Taxonomy meets Global Perspectives.

☑ LESSON IDEA ONLINE 6.5: ASSESSING ABILITY TO ASK AND ANSWER QUESTIONS

Use this lesson idea to encourage students to ask and answer each other's questions and assess their own ability to ask and answer questions. For this lesson idea, you can either give each group the same image or give different images to different groups. You might give all the groups the same topic or you might give images from different topics. It's up to you.

Creating a supportive classroom environment

For any AfL to take place, there has to be a supportive classroom environment, where students feel that they want to progress and achieve. When asking questions, this can be as straightforward as thanking students who respond and then asking if anyone else wants to add anything. Another way of inviting further answers is to use the word 'might' in questions, as in some of the examples given in Table 6.1. This will invite more answers and it doesn't matter if an answer is not completely correct.

Teacher Tip

One way of creating a supportive Global Perspectives classroom is to elicit some ground rules from students at the start of their studies. These can tie in to the spirit and ethos of the subject, in that all perspectives are valid and we should respect other perspectives even if we don't necessarily agree with them. Everyone has a right to be heard without interruption, and we are all reflective learners who guide and support each other.

Summary

In this chapter, we have explored how to make AfL work for you and your students in Global Perspectives lessons.

The key points to remember are:

- AfL in Global Perspectives aims to develop the skills of students rather than to test knowledge.

- AfL is a powerful tool to move students from the level of skill they have achieved now, to where they want to be.

- AfL strategies should be used frequently by Global Perspectives teachers and students to improve learning.

Metacognition

7

What is metacognition?

Metacognition describes the processes involved when students plan, monitor, evaluate and make changes to their own learning behaviours. These processes help students to think about their own learning more explicitly and ensure that they are able to meet a learning goal that they have identified themselves or that we, as teachers, have set.

Metacognitive learners recognise what they find easy or difficult. They understand the demands of a particular learning task and are able to identify different approaches they could use to tackle a problem. Metacognitive learners are also able to make adjustments to their learning as they monitor their progress towards a particular learning goal.

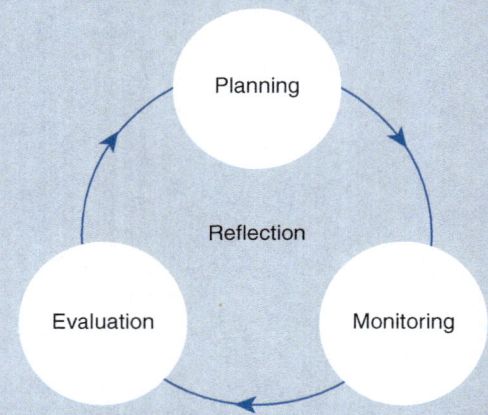

Figure 7.1: A helpful way to think about the phases involved in metacognition.

During the *planning* phase, students think about the explicit learning goal we have set and what we are asking them to do. As teachers, we need to make clear to students what success looks like in any given task before they embark on it. Students build on their prior knowledge, reflect on strategies they have used before and consider how they will approach the new task.

As students put their plan into action, they are constantly *monitoring* the progress they are making towards their learning goal. If the strategies they had decided to use are not working, they may decide to try something different.

Once they have completed the task, students determine how successful the strategy they used was in helping them to achieve their learning goal. During this *evaluation* phase, students think about what went well and what didn't go as well to help them decide what they could do differently next time. They may also think about what other types of problems they could solve using the same strategy.

Reflection is a fundamental part of the plan–monitor–evaluate process and there are various ways in which we can support our students to reflect on their learning process. In order to apply a metacognitive approach, students need access to a set of strategies that they can use and a classroom environment that encourages them to explore and develop their metacognitive skills.

Why teach metacognitive skills?

Research evidence suggests that the use of metacognitive skills plays an important role in successful learning. Metacognitive practices help students to monitor their own progress and take control of their learning. Metacognitive learners think about and learn from their mistakes and modify their learning strategies accordingly. Students who use metacognitive techniques find it improves their academic achievement across subjects, as it helps them transfer what they have learnt from one context to another context, or from a previous task to a new task.

What are the challenges of developing students' metacognitive skills?

For metacognition to be commonplace in the classroom, we need to encourage students to take time to think about and learn from their mistakes. Many students are afraid to make mistakes, meaning that they are less likely to take risks, explore new ways of thinking or tackle unfamiliar problems. We as teachers are instrumental in shaping the culture of learning in a classroom. For metacognitive practices to thrive, students need to feel confident enough to make mistakes, to discuss their mistakes and ultimately to view them as valuable, and often necessary, learning opportunities.

Giving students responsibility for their own learning

In Chapter 3 **The nature of the subject and key considerations**, we explored the kind of subject that Global Perspectives is, and by now, you will understand that much of the learning is directed by the students themselves with initial input, guidance and support from you. In this chapter on metacognition, students investigate strategies to encourage them to understand how they learn best so that they can self-regulate to work independently and collaboratively during their Global Perspectives studies. These strategies give students responsibility for their own learning.

Let's remind ourselves of the skills that Global Perspectives develops: research, analysis, evaluation, reflection, communication and collaboration. Now take a closer look at the phases involved in the metacognition cycle, as presented in the introduction to this chapter.

The phases of metacognition in relation to Global Perspectives

Interestingly, as you will have noticed, we have already come across reflection and evaluation as two of the assessment objectives and skills that Global Perspectives develops. We have explored monitoring in relation to progress in Chapter 6 **Assessment for Learning**. Planning is a skill that needs to be developed just like any other Global Perspectives skill, featuring largely before the completion of any piece of individual work or collaborative project.

Planning

In Chapter 4 **Interpreting a syllabus**, we identified learning objective(s) and success criteria as two of the 'top ten' things to include in your medium-term plan for developing a skill through a global topic. For students to be able to plan how they are going to approach a task, they need to know the learning objective(s) and how they show achievement of them – that is, the success criteria.

Teacher Tip

Learning objectives in Global Perspectives focus on skills. With this in mind, you can refer students back to the last time they met a particular learning objective. You can discuss what the success criteria were then. You can also ask them to think about how they approached the set task and whether this approach was successful or not in achieving the success criteria and meeting the learning objective. Table 7.1 is an example.

Skill	Research
Learning objective	To formulate a research question
Success criteria	To develop questions to consider for research
	To identify where students might find the answers to their research questions
Global topic	Digital world

Table 7.1: Success criteria

Look at the example given for the skill of research. It is likely that students will have come across this learning objective before for a different global topic.

Time spent discussing what the success criteria were then and how they approached achieving them is time well spent. If it's the first time students have met this learning objective, then you could talk them through how they might approach the task and ask for their feedback. Take a look at the section entitled 'Think aloud' later in this chapter for how to do this.

Asking questions

In the planning phase for the example given in the Teacher Tip, you will want to establish what students already know about how to formulate research questions and conduct research. You might use the KWL strategy explored in Chapter 5 **Active learning**. You can also ask questions to help with this.

During the planning phase, students can ask themselves these five questions:

1 What am I supposed to learn?
2 What prior knowledge and understanding will help me to complete this task?
3 What should I do first?
4 What should I be looking for in this text?
5 How much time do I have to complete this task?

☑ LESSON IDEA ONLINE 7.1: APPROACHING ANY TASK

Use this lesson idea to encourage students to think about how they are going to approach a task to meet a set learning objective.

Modelling strategies

Clear learning objectives focus on what students will be able to do by the end of a lesson or series of lessons, and success criteria show students what achievement of a learning objective looks like. Once you have given a learning objective, you can elicit from students what they think are the success criteria.

Teacher Tip

Encourage students to provide you with the success criteria for the learning objective. You can start with easier learning objectives like these:

- To formulate a research question …
- To compare and summarise information from a range of sources …
- To identify a range of perspectives when exploring a global issue …

Once students get used to coming up with success criteria, they should be able to determine the success criteria for more complex learning objectives. For example:

- To actively participate in a range of discussion tasks, demonstrating active listening, giving appropriate information and asking appropriate questions ...

In addition to clear learning objectives and success criteria, you will need to model any strategies you expect students to use for a given task. This modelling may come from you, or it may come from another student. Students showing other students what to do or how to complete a task is effective learning, and you can seize opportunities to empower students to do this in your Global Perspectives lessons. After all, it has been said that the best way of learning something ourselves is to teach it to someone else.

Think aloud

The 'think aloud' approach is exactly that: you or your students saying out loud what you are thinking as you are completing a task. Using the 'think aloud' approach will enable students to experience how they are thinking as well as what they are thinking about. You can model this approach and then encourage students to use it as they are completing tasks that you set.

Teacher Tip

When modelling strategies, keep examples short and clear so that you don't confuse or bore students. You want students to start thinking about their own thinking and learning. They will find it unusual but fun as they start to think aloud and it will help them form good habits for their future learning. Stress that once they are used to the idea, they don't actually need to speak out loud, but can do their thinking aloud in their head. Try this as an example of thinking aloud about how to do some research. You can actually show students what you are doing as you think aloud if you have internet access and your computer is connected to a screen:

'So, I need to find out about the causes and consequences of unemployment. Last time I did research, I started by putting the topic into Google. So, I'll try that ...'

'There are too many results ... wow ... 87 000. I need to narrow my search. I'll start with causes ...'

'That's better, but I might narrow it down further as there are still too many and they are not very specific so I'll add the US as well ... So I have causes of unemployment, and US ...'

'Right, so I need to ignore sites that have 'Ad' – they'll be trying to sell me something, so that's the first two and I don't really want any that are Wikipedia. Leaves a couple that look interesting. I'll try this one.'

☑ LESSON IDEA ONLINE 7.2: THINK ALOUD

Use this lesson idea to encourage your students to think aloud. This lesson idea follows on from the 'think aloud' strategy you modelled for students on how to do research about the causes of unemployment.

Exam wrappers

Another way of having a 'conversation' about learning is using what has become known as the 'exam wrapper' strategy. This strategy is not just suitable for exams, but can work well for any piece of work where you want students to think about and discuss their learning in order to improve their performance. Exam wrappers are short handouts that students complete when a piece of work has been marked and given back to them. These exam wrappers direct students to reflect on their performance based on the feedback the teacher has given so that students know how they might improve their future learning and performance. Lesson idea 7.3 gives an example of how to use an exam wrapper.

☑ LESSON IDEA ONLINE 7.3: EXAM WRAPPER

Use this lesson idea when you want students to have a structured reflective conversation about their learning, so that they can improve their performance. You can use this lesson idea whenever you want a structured opportunity for reflection.

Monitoring

Both you and your students can monitor the progress they are making as they complete a task. By monitoring, you and they can determine whether they are managing to achieve the success criteria or whether they need to try a different strategy. You can 'model' monitoring by circulating around the room and asking individual students the following five questions:

1 How are you doing?
2 What's the next step?
3 Have you used this strategy before?
4 Is this strategy working this time?
5 Do you need to try a different strategy?

Once you have introduced this idea to your class, you could ask them to use the same (slightly rephrased) questions so that they can self-monitor. They could write them inside boxes or speech bubbles and refer to them each time you call out 'self-monitor' during a Global Perspectives lesson.

1 How am I doing?
2 What's my next step?
3 Have I used this strategy before?
4 Is this strategy working this time?
5 Do I need to try a different strategy?

Teacher Tip

Try to encourage your students to do their own monitoring as early as you can in your Global Perspectives course. Find out what your students understand by self-monitoring, the reasons for it and whether they have done self-monitoring before. If the majority of your class knows how to self-monitor, then you can spend time with those that find it more of a challenge. In this way, you will not be rushing round the room trying to ask all students the five questions every time you set a task, and your lesson will be more inclusive. See Chapter 9 **Inclusive education** for more about inclusive education.

☑ LESSON IDEA ONLINE 7.4: WORKING WITH A TEXT

Use this lesson idea to encourage students to self-monitor the progress they are making as they complete the task. You can use any global topic or text for this lesson idea.

Evaluation

Once they have completed a task, you can encourage students to determine the success of the strategy they used in helping them to achieve the learning objective. As seen in Chapter 6 **Assessment for Learning**, during the evaluation phase, students think about what went well and what didn't go so well so that they can plan what to do differently next time they meet the learning objective. Encourage students to reflect at the end of each task, answering the three key questions that follow.

Three key questions to ask

1 What went well?
2 What didn't go so well?
3 What could I do differently next time?

☑ LESSON IDEA ONLINE 7.5: ACTIVE LISTENING

Use this lesson idea for students to evaluate how actively they were listening. This idea can be used at regular intervals during your Global Perspectives course (after a speaking and listening task). By the time they finish, your students will be more active listeners.

Reflection

Reflection is not a phase of the cycle as such, but it is central to the other phases: planning, monitoring and evaluation. Time for reflection allows students time to examine how they are doing and explore whether they need to do something different to improve their performance. One way of getting students to reflect is to ask them to complete a 'reflective journal' of the learning they do and the tasks they complete. You can set aside time after a group activity or an individual piece of writing for students to reflect individually using the 'six steps for reflection' method.

Six steps for reflection

Responding to these six steps will encourage your students to be more reflective.

1 Look back and described what happened (ask students to keep this part short and use the past tense).
2 Think about how what you already know relates to the experience you had (ask students to use the present tense here).
3 Consider how it went (encourage students to include emotions and feelings here and to use the past tense).
4 Explain the parts you think you learnt the most from, why this was and how you and others feel about it (tell students that part of reflection is discussing thoughts and feelings and looking at things from different perspectives).
5 Explain how your thinking about the experience/task/strategy might affect your future learning (encourage students to think about what they might need to do or learn to impact future learning, and to use the future tense as they are predicting).
6 Discuss the experience with others and then reflect further, adding and amending as appropriate.

☑ LESSON IDEA ONLINE 7.6: REFLECTIVE PRACTICE
Use this lesson idea to model how to use the six steps for reflection.

Teacher Tip

Remember, in Global Perspectives you are not teaching the global topics: you are developing skills, and reflection is a skill. By enabling students to reflect in your lessons, you are not only enabling your students to become more effective learners, but also helping your colleagues. Encouraging students to self-question, write a reflective journal and discuss their thought processes with other students are among the ways in which all teachers can encourage students to develop their metacognitive processes. Students will then be better able to work independently and in groups to achieve the learning objectives. Your students and colleagues alike will thank you for the time you spend creating reflective learners.

The aim of teaching metacognitive strategies is to help students become familiar with these strategies so that they use them automatically when completing learning tasks. They will be better able to focus their attention on the task in hand and know how to complete it. They will be able to explain to others what they are doing and how they are doing it. They will also be able to make amendments if something isn't going as planned. Once students are used to thinking about their own learning, they will do it automatically, and when asked what they are doing, they will usually be able to describe their metacognitive processes.

Top tips for encouraging metacognition in Global Perspectives

- Use a metaphor related to Global Perspectives to define what metacognition is.

For example, within the global topic of migration, you can use the metaphor of a long journey. We need to plan where we are going and how we are going to get there. Sometimes we might need to stop and rethink our plans, and change direction. We might come across unforeseen challenges and need to work out how to overcome them by drawing on the knowledge and skills we have. We might even seize opportunities that we weren't expecting as they will help us reach our goal a lot quicker. Whatever we do, we need to keep moving, keeping our goal in focus.

- Whenever possible, give students a choice about the direction in which they want to take their learning.

This is easy to do in Global Perspectives as students have a choice of global topics and can choose their own texts and resources. When they are genuinely interested and motivated to learn about a topic, students will be able to sustain their interest in thinking about a project over a longer time frame. This is essential when working on team projects and research reports, which students will be completing over a number of weeks.

• Model metacognition by talking through mistakes and challenges.

Students learn a lot from listening to their teachers using higher order thinking strategies aloud. Enjoy making mistakes so that students can pick up on these and notice how you stop and correct yourself, showing them that everyone makes mistakes and that these should be seen as learning opportunities.

Summary

In this chapter, we have explored how you can encourage metacognition in your Global Perspectives lessons to create more self-regulated students who take responsibility for their own learning.

Remember:

• Students need to know what the learning objective(s) and success criteria are so that they can plan how to approach a task.

• You need to model strategies that students can use to plan, monitor, evaluate and reflect on how they are learning.

• Make time in your lessons for students to practise becoming more self-regulated learners.

Language awareness

8

What is language awareness?

For many students, English is an additional language. It might be their second or perhaps their third language. Depending on the school context, students might be learning all or just some of their subjects through English.

For all students, regardless of whether they are learning through their first language or an additional language, language is a vehicle for learning. It is through language that students access the learning intentions of the lesson and communicate their ideas. It is our responsibility as teachers to ensure that language doesn't present a barrier to learning.

One way to achieve this is to support our colleagues in becoming more language-aware. Language awareness is sensitivity to, and an understanding of, the language demands of our subject and the role these demands play in learning. A language-aware teacher plans strategies and scaffolds the appropriate support to help students overcome these language demands.

Why is it important for teachers of other subjects to be language-aware?

Many teachers are surprised when they receive a piece of written work that suggests a student who has no difficulties in everyday communication has had problems understanding the lesson. Issues arise when teachers assume that students who have attained a high degree of fluency and accuracy in everyday social English therefore have a corresponding level of academic language proficiency. Whether English is a student's first language or an additional language, students need time and the appropriate support to become proficient in academic language. This is the language that they are mostly exposed to in school and will be required to reproduce themselves. It will also scaffold their ability to access higher order thinking skills and improve levels of attainment.

What are the challenges of language awareness?

Many teachers of non-language subjects worry that there is no time to factor language support into their lessons, or that language is something they know little about. Some teachers may think that language support is not their role. However, we need to work with these teachers to create inclusive classrooms where all students can access the curriculum and where barriers to learning are reduced as much as possible. An increased awareness of the language needs of students aims to reduce any obstacles that learning through an additional language might present.

This doesn't mean that all teachers need to know the names of grammatical structures or need to be able to use the appropriate linguistic labels. What it does mean is that we all need to understand the challenges our students face, including their language level, and plan some strategies to help them overcome these challenges. These strategies do not need to take a lot of additional time and should eventually become integral to our process of planning, teaching and reflecting on our practice. We may need to support other teachers so that they are clear about the vocabulary and language that is specific to their subject, and how to teach, reinforce and develop it.

Becoming more language-aware in Global Perspectives lessons

In Chapter 7 **Metacognition**, you investigated a number of strategies to encourage your Global Perspectives students to think about their learning and how they learn best. One of these is the 'think aloud' strategy introduced in Lesson idea 7.2. This strategy can also be a useful strategy for students who are learning in perhaps their second or third language. While students are thinking aloud, they get to practise functional language, and, while you are wandering around listening, you can determine the help students need to use language for this purpose.

Furthermore, the 'thinking aloud' strategy can support students who are struggling with difficult concepts such as perspectives, evaluation and reflection, as we saw in Chapter 3 **The nature of the subject and key considerations**. Using strategies like the 'think aloud' strategy enables your Global Perspectives lessons to become more inclusive. Ideas for strategies to engage all students in your Global Perspectives lessons are explored further in Chapter 9 **Inclusive education**.

While many of the lesson ideas in this book can be used for a variety of purposes, this chapter focuses specifically on how you can become more language-aware in your Global Perspectives lessons. It includes the following:

- your role as the teacher
- use of visuals
- listening and speaking
- reading and writing
- examination-specific vocabulary.

Your role as the teacher

If you are a speaker of English as a second or third language yourself, you may already be aware of the difficulties posed by communicating in a foreign language. If not, you may have tried at some point to learn another language and are only too aware of how difficult this can be. Think about the times you have failed to communicate because of a language barrier. Remember these times in your Global Perspectives lessons. Your students will thank you for empathising with them and creating opportunities to help them achieve the learning objective(s).

As teachers, it's important for us to recognise that what we do is key to helping students with the language they need to meet set learning objectives. There are a number of things you can do to ensure that the language of learning (English in the case of Global Perspectives courses) does not become a barrier to skill development.

Teacher Tip

You might try asking your colleagues how they help their students with language development. As Global Perspectives is a transdisciplinary subject, you will probably find that other subject teachers such as English Language, Geography and Social Science teachers might already have word lists defining key terminology in English for their subject. For example, your students may already be familiar with geographical terms such as 'sustainability', 'climate change' and 'global warming', and with vocabulary such as 'biodiversity' and 'ecosystem loss' from Science lessons. Another way of establishing the key vocabulary students already know in relation to a global topic is to ask students to work in small groups to brainstorm.

☑ LESSON IDEA ONLINE 8.1: BRAINSTORMING

Use this lesson idea to establish rules for brainstorming and at the start of a new global topic to find out what vocabulary students already know about the topic. You can then compile a list of key vocabulary that students can refer to if need be as lessons progress.

Planning lessons that show language awareness

Being more language-aware means planning for the language that students need in your lessons. You might not always know what language that will be, but you do know the learning objective(s), the global topic and the resources you will be using, so you can certainly plan for some of it. Asking yourself some key questions, as in Figure 8.1, will help you plan how you can support your students with language.

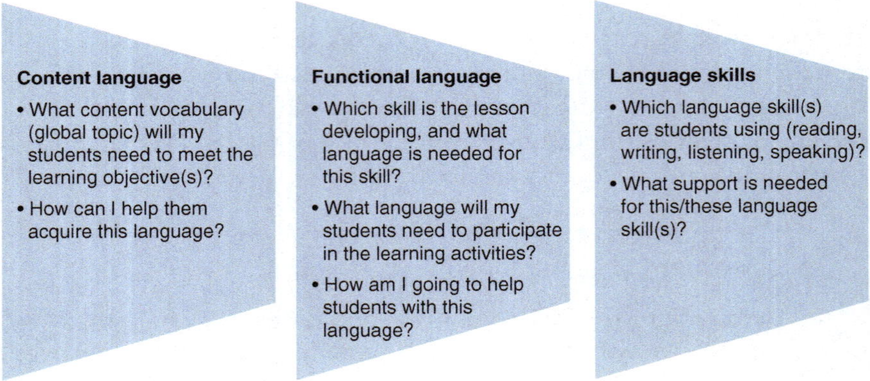

Content language
- What content vocabulary (global topic) will my students need to meet the learning objective(s)?
- How can I help them acquire this language?

Functional language
- Which skill is the lesson developing, and what language is needed for this skill?
- What language will my students need to participate in the learning activities?
- How am I going to help students with this language?

Language skills
- Which language skill(s) are students using (reading, writing, listening, speaking)?
- What support is needed for this/these language skill(s)?

Figure 8.1: Planning for language awareness in Global Perspectives lessons.

Teacher Tip

It's a good idea to get used to adding as much of the language students will need as you can foresee to your lesson plans. For example, consider the following: learning outcome, learning objective (skill-focused), success criteria, learning activity and resources:

Learning outcome: Produce a poster to persuade of the importance of learning another language in school.

Learning objective: Select the most important information gathered from a range of sources, and identify and explain key issues within the topic (the skill here is analysis).

Success criteria: Read information from web-based sources and draw conclusions about where languages are spoken and by how many people.

You might have been thinking about the language students will need as you read through the details of the lesson. It will be something like this …

Content vocabulary: Languages, foreign, additional, community, names of countries, travel, employment, communication, misunderstandings, barriers, loss, media, traditions, cultures, societies.

Functional language: Language of persuasion, for example, if I were you, I suggest, it's important that, obviously, clearly we need to, is a must, the point is, that's the reason why, another reason, a real must.

Language skill: Reading.

Support for language skill: Use of dictionaries and a word list generated from the brainstorm activity at the start of the lesson.

Another way of supporting students with language is often referred to as 'pre-teaching'. Pre-teaching the vocabulary students will need in a lesson will enable them to complete necessary tasks without having to constantly stop to look up vocabulary in their dictionaries or ask you for the meaning of words. For Global Perspectives, you might find it useful to spend some time at the end of a lesson telling students what they will be doing in the next lesson. You can give them a worksheet with a couple of vocabulary activities such as a word association activity, a gap fill or a wordsearch to practise the vocabulary they will need in that lesson. In fact, wordsearches are a great way of revising vocabulary. Ask students to create them and swap with a partner to find the answers. Encourage students to add clues so that their partners know what words to look for.

☑ LESSON IDEA ONLINE 8.2: PRE-TEACHING VOCABULARY

You can use this lesson idea with any vocabulary that you might want students to be familiar with for a Global Perspectives lesson.

Teacher Tip

Give students a worksheet with useful functional language on it. They can use this language in their spoken and written work. Words like 'if …' and 'then …' are useful for describing cause and effect. 'On the other hand', 'however', 'in addition', 'nevertheless', 'in spite of', 'despite' and 'although' can all be used for speaking and writing during Global Perspectives lessons; for example, in debates and discussions, for presentations, as well as for producing summaries and written arguments. 'Strengths', 'limitations' and 'improvements' are useful words for reflection and evaluation.

Use of visuals

Visuals are a great way of supporting language acquisition. Body language, gestures and visuals including photographs, charts, graphs, video clips and diagrams all help students with understanding. You can make any text more accessible by adding visuals to it. Consider the following example.

Text A

Climate change can have devastating effects. The effects depend on where you live. For example, there have been severe droughts in some parts of the world. Meanwhile, other places are experiencing flooding to such an extent that people are displaced and may not be able to return to their homes for many months. They find themselves living in community centres with other families and dependent on charities for warm clothing and food.

Text B

Climate change can have devastating effects. The effects depend on where you live. For example, there have been severe droughts in some parts of the world.

Meanwhile, other places are experiencing flooding to such an extent that people are displaced and may not be able to return to their home for many months.

Whole families find themselves living in community centres with other families, dependent on charities for warm clothing and food.

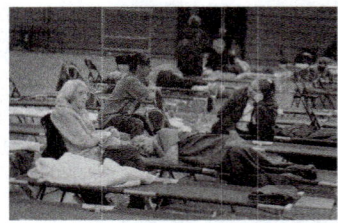

As you will have noticed, despite being almost exactly the same text, Text B is easier to understand than Text A due to the supporting visuals.

☑ LESSON IDEA ONLINE 8.3: USING VISUALS 1

Use this lesson idea before using any text, written or spoken, to encourage students to think about and produce the language that they might need to access the text.

Listening and speaking

Listening can be a challenging skill as students generally lack control of the recording unless they have headphones and are able to access the recording as many times as they need. This is not always possible or desirable as you might want the whole class to be listening to the same recording at the same time. Due to the nature of the subject, as explored in Chapter 3 **The nature of the subject and key considerations**, you will probably use short extracts from films and video clips quite often in your Global Perspectives lessons. Even though the visuals will support students' understanding, some students might find that the speed of the speech in the clips prevents them from understanding everything. So, depending on the level of the students, you could also put subtitles on the video clip. This will enable students to make connections between the pronunciation and the spelling, and to understand more of what is happening within the video.

Teacher Tip

Before listening to texts, you might want to do some pre-listening activities. For example, you can ask students to predict what the text will be about and the content and type of text from the title. You can also ask them to write down words and short phrases that they think they will hear. Identifying what you want students to gain from listening to the text can also support understanding, once students listen.

Use headings like: 'Issue', 'Cause', 'Consequence', 'Solution', and so on. Students then make notes under these headings rather than having to listen and understand every word they hear. Pause the video clip at key moments to allow students to think and write under their headings. Keep video clips short: no more than 15 minutes, as students will tire and lose focus if the clip is longer.

☑ LESSON IDEA ONLINE 8.4: USING VISUALS 2

Use this lesson idea to support your students' listening and speaking. You can use any listening text or global topic.

When introducing any listening or speaking activity, it's important that you make it clear what you want students to do and why. You should show students what success looks and sounds like. You'll find more about learning objectives and success criteria in Chapter 5 **Active learning** and Chapter 6 **Assessment for Learning**. You might also clarify that students have understood the task by asking questions like:

- What have I asked you to do?
- Why have I asked you to do it?
- What does success in this task look/sound like?

Teacher Tip

Make speaking and listening activities relevant to students' experience by using photos taken by you or them to discuss local issues that have global significance. Encourage students to discuss local issues such as wasting water (a photo of a swimming pool or a green on a golf course), environmental pollution (a power station or traffic fumes) and animals for entertainment (tourists on a camel or an elephant). Ask students to listen to local news reports on the television. These can be in students' first language. Once they have watched the local news report, they can tell the class what it was about, in English. By doing this, students can switch between their first language and English. They can use dictionaries to look up unfamiliar words and use their own words and phrases to get the message across, thereby avoiding plagiarism.

Reading and writing

Words are the basis of any language. The more familiar a student is with the words in a text, the easier it will be for a student to understand what the text is about. It's also important to stress that students don't need to know and understand every word to be able to access the text and that, often, they will be skimming and scanning texts to look for relevance or for specific information.

Teacher Tip

It's important that there is a purpose for reading, for example, for gist (skimming), for detail (scanning), to acquire new vocabulary, to develop their own ideas, or to gather evidence.

Ask your students whether they know the difference between skimming and scanning, and the purpose of each. If they don't, then you or another student in your class can explain and/or exemplify the difference. By doing this, you can make reading a lot more accessible for all students.

☑ LESSON IDEA ONLINE 8.5: READING TEXT ANALYSIS

Use this lesson idea with any reading text on a global topic or issue to explore the difference between skimming and scanning.

You might like to give students a glossary of key words in their first and second language. This works well, for example, if you are teaching in a context where all students speak one first language, but it might not be realistic if you have a multilingual class with a mixture of first languages. In this case, you could use images as a way of explaining meaning.

Additionally, you might give all students a list of vocabulary relevant to the global topic in English and ask them to work in pairs to explain the words to each other. You can make a game of it by telling students to explain the word in English without mentioning the word on the list. You can then elicit and check these meanings with the whole class. This shows students that they can use other words, as long as they communicate.

Teacher Tip

You can have your own dictionary available and model its use. Whenever students come across a new word, make it obvious that they should refer to their dictionary. Students will only become independent learners if they are able to learn on their own. If you tell them the meaning of every new word, they will come to rely on you and not bother looking up words for themselves, making them dependent rather than independent.

When you ask students whose first language is not English to write something in English, there are two key processes that they have to go through. The first is to think of a response to the question(s) or title of the piece of work you want them to do. The second is to find the words. Students might find it easier to respond to the task in their first language before putting their response into English. Encouraging students to plan what they write will help them to produce their response using the correct vocabulary.

☑ LESSON IDEA ONLINE 8.6: PLANNING A RESPONSE

Use this lesson idea to give students the opportunity to plan out their response. You can use it for any activity where you want students to produce either a written or a spoken response.

To support students' writing, you can also use sentence starters and writing frames. Some useful sentence starters for Global Perspectives include:

- … is a serious local issue, because …
- There are many causes, one being that …
- The most likely reason for this is …
- The consequences include …

- One course of action might be to …
- As a result of …
- We can draw the conclusion that …
- There is reliable evidence to show that …
- The evidence demonstrates …
- According to …

A writing frame can be made up of sub-headings, as in the example in Figure 8.2.

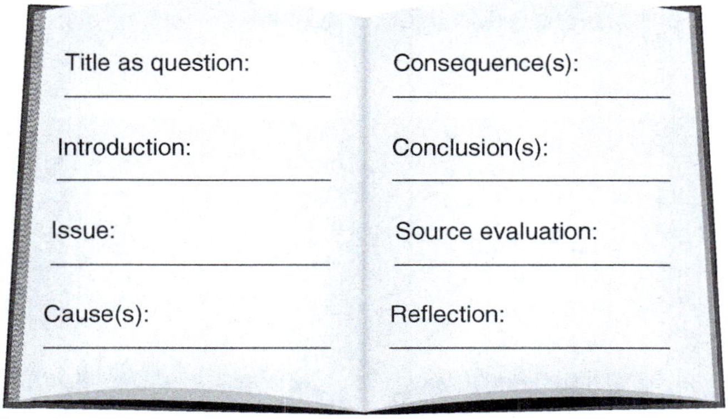

Figure 8.2

Examination-specific vocabulary

For written examinations, certain words are used in place of direct questions to indicate the type of answer required. These are known as 'command words'. For example, if students are asked to 'identify' a cause, which attracts only one mark, they should look in the relevant source material and simply pick out one cause and write it down. They do not need to change the vocabulary, but won't lose marks if they do as long as they answer the question. The command word here is 'identify'.

Top ten command words for Global Perspectives written examinations

1 Analyse
2 Assess
3 Compare
4 Evaluate
5 Explain

6   Give
7   Name
8   Identify
9   Justify
10 Respond.

☑ LESSON IDEA ONLINE 8.7: COMMAND WORDS

Use this lesson idea as a quick starter activity to ensure that students know what the command words mean, before giving them some written examination practice.

Summary

In this chapter, we have explored how you can be more language-aware and help your students with language in your Global Perspectives lessons so that language does not become a barrier to learning.

Remember:

- Plan for language support by including content vocabulary, functional language and support for language skills in your lesson plans.

- Adapt texts by simplifying the language or adding visuals.

- Provide a language-rich environment by using all four skills: listening, speaking, reading and writing.

Inclusive
education

9

What is inclusive education?

Individual differences among students will always exist; our challenge as teachers is to see these not as problems to be fixed but as opportunities to enrich and make learning accessible for all. Inclusion is an effort to make sure all students receive whatever specially designed instruction and support they need to succeed as learners.

An inclusive teacher welcomes all students and finds ways to accept and accommodate each individual student. An inclusive teacher identifies existing barriers that limit access to learning, then finds solutions and strategies to remove or reduce those barriers. Some barriers to inclusion are visible; others are hidden or difficult to recognise.

Barriers to inclusion might be the lack of educational resources available for teachers or an inflexible curriculum that does not take into account the learning differences that exist among all learners, across all ages. We also need to encourage students to understand each others' barriers, or this itself may become a barrier to learning.

Students may experience challenges because of any one or a combination of the following:

- behavioural and social skill difficulties
- communication or language disabilities
- concentration difficulties
- conflict in the home or that caused by political situations or national emergency
- executive functions, such as difficulties in understanding, planning and organising
- hearing impairments, acquired congenitally or through illness or injury
- literacy and language difficulties
- numeracy difficulties
- physical or neurological impairments, which may or may not be visible
- visual impairments, ranging from mild to severe.

We should be careful, however, not to label a student and create further barriers in so doing, particularly if we ourselves are not qualified to make a diagnosis. Each child is unique but it is our management of their learning environment that will decide the extent of the barrier and the need for it to be a factor. We need to be aware of a child's readiness to learn and their readiness for school.

Why is inclusive education important?

Teachers need to find ways to welcome all students and organise their teaching so that each student gets a learning experience that makes engagement and success possible. We should create a good match between what we teach and how we teach it, and what the student needs and is capable of. We need not only to ensure access but also make sure each student receives the support and individual attention that result in meaningful learning.

What are the challenges of an inclusive classroom?

Some students may have unexpected barriers. Those who consistently do well in class may not perform in exams, or those who are strong at writing may be weaker when speaking. Those who are considered to be the brightest students may also have barriers to learning. Some students may be working extra hard to compensate for barriers they prefer to keep hidden; some students may suddenly reveal limitations in their ability to learn, using the techniques they have been taught. We need to be aware of all corners of our classroom, be open and put ourselves in our students' shoes.

Making Global Perspectives lessons more inclusive

Our focus in Chapter 8 **Language awareness** was on how you might help your students that don't have English as their first language to access your Global Perspectives lessons using a variety of strategies.

In this chapter, you will be able to add to your range of strategies to support all students in your Global Perspectives lessons at a level that is appropriately challenging for them. We will be exploring how you can:

- respond to the multiple intelligences of your students to help promote inclusive learning
- use Bloom as a method of differentiation
- provide choice to encourage inclusivity.

Responding to students' multiple intelligences to promote inclusive learning

The theory of multiple intelligences as outlined by Gardner in 1993 is *one* approach or framework that can be helpful for all teachers when thinking about how to make lessons more inclusive. It offers a useful tool for you to think about the different ways in which students process information and access learning. However, it's important that students aren't labelled as a particular 'intelligence'. Investigating Gardner's (1993) multiple intelligences in depth is beyond the scope of this book, although you can find reference to his work in the bibliography should you wish to delve deeper. Needless to say, when considering how you might make your Global Perspectives lessons more inclusive, it's important to reflect on the talents and aptitudes of your students. This is in addition to considering the skill you want to develop, as well as the learning intention and the type of task you want students to undertake, as demonstrated by Table 9.1.

In Table 9.1, you can see how aptitude or intelligence is defined by different skills and different tasks. By understanding that students have multiple intelligences, you will be able to provide a variety of stimulating activities that cater for the combination of intelligences present in your classroom. Being aware of these intelligences can provide a framework for offering a choice of relevant activities, which might better meet the needs of all your students.

Intelligence	Defined by...	Type of task
Verbal-linguistic	spoken, written language	writing poems, news articles, newsletters, speeches/discussions/ debates, designing checklists, research, taking notes
Visual-spatial	non-verbal, images, graphs, charts	posters, mind maps (with visuals), photo stimulus, cartoons, highlighting
Musical	listening, sounds	songs and rhythms for memory, synthesis and summary using sound
Logical-mathematical	problem-solving, critical thinking, drawing conclusions	interpreting graphs, surveys, organising information, timelines, advantages/ disadvantages
Natural-linguistic	interest in topics such as biodiversity and ecosystem loss, humans and other species, and so on	fieldtrips, photo collage, photo journal, descriptions of local/ global environments
Bodily-kinesthetic	hands-on activities, experiential learning	video recordings, role play, drama sketch, gestures, creating puzzles
Interpersonal	understanding people, communicative, collaborative	weblog, reflecting on group's learning, evaluating strengths and limitations, suggesting improvements, interviews, leading discussions, group and pair work, brainstorming
Intrapersonal	understand themselves, independent learning, planning	weblog, reflecting on own learning, evaluating strengths and limitations, setting goals

Table 9.1: Multiple intelligences meet in the context of Global Perspectives.

Teacher Tip

If you are an experienced teacher of Global Perspectives, you will no doubt have tried lots of different strategies to engage your students. You might have been puzzled why one activity works well for one student but not for another. Multiple intelligences could explain this.

For example, let's imagine that you gave your students the task of producing something to explain the causes and consequences of globalisation. Think about what your students might have produced.

If they produced a poem or news article, they showed verbal-linguistic intelligence. If they created a song set to music, they displayed musical intelligence. They may have used charts and graphs to explain their research findings, showing evidence of logical-mathematical intelligence, and so on.

Your classroom would have been alive with all your students creating something different. You might have found that some wanted to work together, and were happy for them to do so.

On the other hand, if you had asked all your students to produce a poem, your classroom might have felt very different as the narrowness of this task might have failed to provide the opportunity for multiple intelligences to thrive. Students who have literacy and language difficulties might not have been able to access this task, whereas, given a choice, students could produce a different response such as a numerical one in the form of a graph to explain their research findings.

☑ LESSON IDEA ONLINE 9.1: MULTIPLE INTELLIGENCES

Use this lesson idea to get students to self-assess their own aptitudes and realise why they find some activities more challenging than others. If you and your students know what their barriers to learning are, you can adapt your teaching to try to overcome these barriers.

Bloom's Revised Taxonomy as one method of differentiation

In Chapter 6 **Assessment for Learning**, we reflected on some of the questions we can ask students using Bloom's Revised Taxonomy. Directing different levels of question at different students helps support inclusion in that you can challenge some students with higher order thinking questions, commonly known as HOTs. You can also use lower order thinking questions, or LOTs, for those students that need them, or at times when you are perhaps starting a new topic or using an image as a stimulus. The questions might start with a LOT, for example, 'What is the issue?' You might then increase the difficulty by asking a HOT, for example, 'Why do you think it's an issue?'

Teacher Tip

When questioning, a good way of including all students is to ask questions with the word 'might' in them, so that no answer can be completely wrong and you can invite many responses. For example, 'What might the issue be?' is still a LOT, but you will get a lot more responses. In fact, it will be more like a brainstorming session than a direct question-and-answer session. Similarly, 'Why might this be an issue?' is still a HOT, but it allows for more responses from more students who will have a go at answering it. Asking questions in this way makes your lesson more inclusive.

You can also use Bloom's Revised Taxonomy to add to the tasks for different multiple intelligences to make them more complex as they factor in critical thinking skills (analysis, synthesis, evaluation). Table 9.2 gives some examples.

Another way of using Bloom's Revised Taxonomy in Global Perspectives lessons is to design tasks aimed at the different levels of the hierarchy: remembering, understanding, applying, analysing, evaluating and creating. You can then either assign particular tasks to students or allow students to choose their own tasks. Students might even work through tasks from the lower level to the higher level of the taxonomy. Some of the tasks could be done at home and others in class.

Intelligence	Task	Addressing critical thinking skills
Verbal-linguistic	Write three headlines that you might find in *The Futuristic Times*	showing your understanding of how technology might impact global society in the future *(analysis)*
Visual-spatial	Create a cartoon strip	exploring the impact of the Olympic games *(synthesis)*
Musical	Create a rap song	explaining the advantages and disadvantages of globalisation *(analysis/synthesis)*
Logical-mathematical	Create a puzzle (wordsearch, crossword, jigsaw)	comparing the causes and effects of migration *(analysis)*
Natural-linguistic	Create a photo journal	distinguishing between the treatment of animals, locally and globally *(synthesis/analysis)*
Bodily-kinesthetic	Produce a video clip	raising awareness about keeping fit and healthy *(application/synthesis)*
Interpersonal	Produce an outcome (video clip, presentation, lesson plan) in a group	informing others about how stereotyping influences our interactions with others *(synthesis/analysis)*
Intrapersonal	Write a weblog (reflective piece of writing)	learning about own learning and work processes in, and contributions to, a team project *(evaluation/synthesis/analysis)*

Table 9.2: Multiple intelligences with critical thinking skills.

☑ LESSON IDEA ONLINE 9.2: TIC-TAC-TOE CHOICE BOARD
Use this lesson idea as a way of using Bloom's Revised Taxonomy for different levels of task.

Once you have tried Lesson idea 9.2, you will see how engaged your students are as they have been allowed to choose the way they are learning (within the parameters that you have set) and do things that they are good at. This is good practice and Global Perspectives is the ideal subject for you to be able to use choice boards, as in Lesson idea 9.2.

Learning menus encourage inclusive learning

As seen when looking at multiple intelligences earlier in the chapter, all your Global Perspectives students have different strengths and talents. One way of capitalising on this is to offer students a choice of learning activities to enable them to meet the set learning objective(s), as you did in Lesson idea 9.2. You can also present this choice of activities as a learning menu.

Learning menus

A learning menu is a collection of independent learning activities, presented in a 'menu' layout. There are many benefits to learning menus.

Learning menus:

- provide choice so that students can do something of interest and/or that they have an aptitude for
- help to overcome any barriers to learning that might exist, such as concentration difficulties or difficulties in planning and organising, as students have to plan and organise how to complete an activity of their choice
- encourage the development of independent thinking
- provide challenge for students as they promote higher level thinking.

☑ LESSON IDEA ONLINE 9.3: LEARNING MENU

Use this lesson idea for any global topic to give a *menu* of activities for your Global Perspectives students.

Teacher Tip

Even though choice boards and learning menus take some time to prepare, they are well worth the effort and you can reuse them for different global topics and issues. You can also swap them with colleagues who have created different choice boards and learning menus. If you have another look at the tic-tac-toe choice board you used for Lesson idea 9.2 and the learning menu in Lesson idea 9.3, you will see that you can adapt the tasks for any global topic or issue. Preparing these, therefore, is good use of your time. You can also ask students to help create them. For example, you can list all the skills on the board – remembering, understanding, applying, analysing, evaluating, creating – and ask students to brainstorm different tasks for the different skills. They could do this in small groups, with each group brainstorming one skill. You will then have a ready-made list for all of Bloom's levels.

Choice boards and learning menus are ideal for independent learning in Global Perspectives lessons, but just because they work well doesn't mean we should use them all the time. Like all good teaching, in Global Perspectives lessons we should try to use a variety of activities to meet the learning objective(s). Sometimes this will mean enabling students to work in pairs and small groups.

Using groups to support learning and achievement

You have already tried one excellent way of getting students to work and learn together in groups when you used the jigsaw strategy in Chapter 5 **Active learning**, Lesson idea 5.9. The jigsaw strategy enables individual students, including some who may have behavioural or social skill difficulties, to be supported by group members, and is therefore a strategy you can use to make your Global Perspectives lessons more inclusive. In this section, we will explore three further strategies that enable students to be supported by you and their peers.

These strategies are:

1 half-class/half-class
2 making connections
3 numbered heads together.

1 Half-class/half-class

As its name suggests, this strategy can be used when one half of the class is working independently, perhaps using a choice board or learning menu, or completing some form of peer or self-assessment, for example giving feedback on a partner's work. The other half can then work in a smaller group with you. This allows you to ask questions to identify anyone that is struggling and to clarify any misunderstandings. After 10–15 minutes, you can then do the same with the other half of the class.

You can even make the groups smaller and have three groups. By doing this, you can respond more easily to the differing needs of your students, allowing you to make your lessons more inclusive.

Teacher Tip

Try not to be discouraged if the half-class/half-class or small group strategy doesn't work the first time you use it. Students need to get used to the idea of working independently, organising themselves to start work straight away, knowing that you are not there to answer every question they have. You will need to manage the class so that students can work independently: give them tasks they can do without your help. As well as learning menus and choice boards, you can ask students to write a reflection on what they learnt in the last lesson. They can make a KWL chart for one of the global topics (see Chapter 5 **Active learning**). They can also read and highlight facts, opinions, perspectives, issues, causes, effects, and so on, from a text, or do some research while you are working with the other group.

---

2   Making connections

Students can work with a partner for this strategy. By making connections, students can synthesise their understanding of a particular topic or issue using a combination of words and pictures. Encourage students to group ideas, write and answer questions, or write definitions and give examples, which they label accordingly. If students use coloured markers and sticky notes, they will be able to produce a great visual aid for review at a later stage. You might pair students according to their multiple intelligences and/or take their linguistic ability into account. You will need to provide each student with ten sticky notes, and each pair with coloured markers and a large sheet of paper, each time you want them to do this activity. Lesson idea 9.4 practises using this strategy.

☑ LESSON IDEA ONLINE 9.4: MAKING CONNECTIONS

Use this lesson idea to allow students to work in pairs to make connections to create a visual representation of their learning and achievement. You can use any global topic or issue for this.

Teacher Tip

You may find that some students find it difficult to come up with key words, questions and phrases on their own for the making connections activity in Lesson idea 9.4. If they are paired with someone who knows some key words and phrases for the topic, then there is no problem. However, you might not always be aware of this at the start of the activity so you need another strategy. You can scaffold students' learning by giving them a list of key terms, questions and phrases. Students then work with their partner to organise and group these terms, questions and phrases, adding examples with labels on them.

---

3 Numbered heads together

Like many of the strategies in this book, this one can be used with any Global Perspectives students to, for example, answer a question, solve a puzzle, or create an awareness campaign about an issue.

Each member of the group is given a number, depending on the number in the group. For example, if you have small groups of four, members will be numbered one, two, three and four. Groups work together on the task by putting their heads together. Everyone in the group needs to know what the answer is or be able to present to the rest of the class, as no one knows who will be asked. Once you have given students enough time, ask one number (for example, all the number threes) from each group, one at a time, to give an answer or come up to the board to write a definition, and so on. Each correct answer can be awarded a point to the groups that get it right to add an element of competition. Remember to have a smiley sticker or small reward ready for the winning team. I like to give novelty pens, pencils and erasers as small prizes for competitive tasks.

Teacher Tip

There is a difference between students working *in* a group and students working *as* a group. Working in a group often means that students are doing independent work but are sitting in groups. When they work *as* a group, on the other hand, such as in the 'numbered heads together' strategy, you will have mixed ability groups, and, even though some will finish the task more quickly than others, you can tell students that you expect them to support each other so that everyone knows how to complete the task. Try asking students to prepare a three- or four-slide presentation about a global issue where each member of the group takes responsibility for producing one slide (for example, the causes and consequences of biodiversity and ecosystem loss and possible courses of action would work for a group of three). Once one member has completed their slide, they should help the others complete theirs. As a group, they should then reflect on what they have produced and highlight two stars and one wish for developing their presentation further.

Even though you are creating independent learners by giving your students choice and enabling them to work in groups for support, there may be times when students have to do things that they feel they are not so good at or have little aptitude for. Point out to students that we all have to do things we find difficult, but that we can challenge ourselves to do them as well as we can. For example, writing a 2000-word research report in English is going to be a challenge for some students, but giving them short practice research and writing tasks and encouraging students to keep notes from their research will help. When creating learning activities, you need to keep the assessment objectives (research, analysis, evaluation, reflection, communication and collaboration) in mind as these dictate what students have to do for the summative assessment of their Global Perspectives course. If the learning objectives and success criteria are clear, you can provide appropriately challenging learning activities that will motivate all your students, leading them to success at the end of their Global Perspectives course.

Summary

In this chapter, we have focused on making your Global Perspectives lessons more inclusive so that all your students are engaged and appropriately challenged.

Remember:

- Give students a choice of learning activities to meet their learning needs and preferences and to enable them to become more independent learners.

- Students have different aptitudes, which might explain why they find some tasks more challenging than others. Encourage them not just to choose tasks where their talents lie, but also to challenge themselves by completing tasks that they may have less of an aptitude for.

- Make learning activities more demanding by adding critical thinking skills to tasks, and support students' learning by enabling them to work in pairs and in small groups.

Teaching with digital technologies

10

What are digital technologies?

Digital technologies enable our students to access a wealth of up-to-date digital resources, collaborate locally and globally, curate existing material and create new material. They include electronic devices and tools that manage and manipulate information and data.

Why use digital technologies in the classroom?

When used successfully, digital technologies have the potential to transform teaching and learning. The effective use of technology in the classroom encourages active learning, knowledge construction, inquiry and exploration among students. It should enhance an existing task or provide opportunities to do things that could not be done without it. It can also enhance the role of assessment, providing new ways for students to demonstrate evidence of learning.

New technologies are redefining relationships and enabling new opportunities. But there are also risks, so we should encourage our students to be knowledgeable about and responsible in their use of technology. Integrating technology into our teaching helps prepare students for a future rooted in an increasingly digitised world.

What are the challenges of using digital technologies?

The key to ensuring that technology is used effectively is to remember that it is simply a resource, and not an end in itself. As with the use of all resources, the key is not to start with the resource itself, but to start with what you want the student to learn. We need to think carefully about why and how to use technologies as well as evaluating their efficiency and effectiveness.

If students are asked to use digital technologies as part of their homework, it is important that all students are able to access the relevant technology outside school. A school needs to think about a response to any 'digital divide', because if technology is 'adding value', then all students need to be able to benefit. Some schools choose to make resources available to borrow or use in school, or even loan devices to students.

Safety for students and teachers is a key challenge for schools and it is important to consider issues such as the prevention of cyber-bullying, the hacking of personal information, access to illegal or banned materials and distractions from learning. As technology changes, schools and teachers need to adapt and implement policies and rules.

One of the greatest pitfalls is for a teacher to feel that they are not skilled technologists, and therefore not to try. Creative things can be done with simple technology, and a highly effective teacher who knows very little about technology can often achieve much more than a less effective teacher who is a technology expert. Knowing how to use technology is not the same as knowing how to teach with it.

Using technology as a tool in the Global Perspectives classroom

In my experience, some teachers shy away from using technology in the classroom for fear of breaking equipment or simply not knowing how to use technology in lessons, even though they use it for their own purposes and know that their teaching and students' learning might gain some benefit from using it. This chapter focuses on the benefits of using technology for Global Perspectives. You will investigate how you can use it for effective teaching, effective learning, as an aid for Assessment for Learning and to increase inclusivity in your Global Perspectives lessons.

Using technology for effective teaching

Without effective teaching in the classroom, effective learning is unlikely to happen. What we as teachers do impacts our students' learning. We have already discussed how having clear learning objectives is key to helping students know where they are trying to get to. You or they can determine how they get there, and that's where technology comes in. You can look at technology as a tool, just like any other, for example a textbook or a worksheet. There is a plethora of different technologies available, so, rather than naming too many specifics, we will explore how you can use technology first for effective teaching.

Access to resources

One of the key benefits of technology for the Global Perspectives teacher is the availability of high-quality resources for you to use with your students. As Global Perspectives focuses on global topics and issues within these topics, which can change at an alarming rate, it's great to know that we can gain real-time resources – for example, up-to-date news clips, images and interviews.

Teacher Tip

Rather than trying to search for hundreds of different video clips from different websites, use a few websites that you know are reliable. Try the following to build up a bank of video clips for the global topics you have decided to focus on to develop your students' skills.

As well as YouTube video clips, the top three websites for video clips about global issues are:

1 Global Issues
2 TED
3 True Tube

You can assign students a homework task of finding one useful video clip (no longer than ten minutes) that is relevant to the global topic you are exploring at the time.

LESSON IDEA ONLINE 10.1: SOURCING AND EVALUATING INFORMATION

Use this lesson idea for any global topic to focus on the development of the skills of research and evaluation, both of which are Global Perspectives assessment objectives.

Connecting with others

As well as accessing resources – video clips and spoken and written texts – digital technology can be used to connect with others from all over the world. This is a real bonus for Global Perspectives students as they can easily connect with others to find out different perspectives about an issue. Here are three different ways you can facilitate this.

1 Via email. If you have a link with schools in different parts of the world, students can send questionnaires and links to surveys to find out different cultural perspectives. The advantage of email is that it is asynchronous, in that it doesn't matter when students send their emails as they don't need to connect with others at the same time.

2 Via a video conferencing system. Students could prepare questions to ask students in another Global Perspectives lesson in a different part of the world. Video conferences can be recorded and played back at a later date for students to make notes, and students can extend their conversations as they think of questions. The drawback is that this is synchronous communication, which requires students to be online at the same time.

3   Via social media. Similar to email, social media has the advantage of being asynchronous and you can set up a closed group so that only those you have invited can access the group. As well as sharing documents and surveys, you can also share images and sources of information. Blogs can be a useful way of gaining insight into other cultures and enabling students to become more reflective.

Cambridge Online Learning Area

Cambridge International Examinations offer an Online Learning Area with extensive materials specifically for Global Perspectives. This is freely available to all Cambridge centres delivering or considering delivery of Global Perspectives.

This Online Learning Area provides online structured courses, with guidance for both students and teachers, and multimedia resources, together with teaching and learning activities. Secure personal journals encourage higher-level thinking among students as they engage with and reflect on the materials and activities. Spaces with forum discussions allow for collaboration opportunities in a range of ways including between schools, in topic-based groups and within students' own class groups. Teachers can also collaborate with other Global Perspectives teachers in different parts of the world.

Students can use ePortfolio tools to gather together, share their research and gain feedback from peers and teachers.

Teachers and students can access the Online Learning Area using any connected device, including tablets, laptops and desktop machines. If teachers request student accounts, the area also supports flipped learning opportunities, providing students with access outside the traditional classroom environment.

Teachers can register for an account on the Cambridge International Examinations website.

Teacher Tip

When using the internet for connecting with others, it's important to refer to the school's internet safety policy and take simple precautions to protect the identity of students. Try to explore ways of connecting that don't require students to give out their personal details. For example, a school email account might be used. You can use social media websites that are specifically designed for schools. A great one is Edmodo. One feature of Edmodo is that students don't need email accounts to log in.

☑ **LESSON IDEA ONLINE 10.2: CONNECTING WITH OTHERS**
Use this lesson idea to gain different cultural perspectives about any global topic or issue.

Using technology for effective student learning

As we have seen so far in this chapter, technology offers students a way of learning anywhere, at any time and with anyone. It can act as a motivator for tasks that students might previously have found boring, such as writing an essay or producing a poster. Alternatives that use technology might be a short video clip or a photo journal.

You don't have to be a technology expert to start using digital technologies to improve student learning. Encouraging students to use Word processing for writing instead of paper and pen is a step in the right direction. Word processing enables students to start writing without having to think about the structure immediately. For example, they can move sections around, add an introduction at a later date or start with a conclusion. Word-processing software (such as Word) is also useful for personalised feedback from peers and from you as the teacher. See more about this in the section entitled 'Using technology for Assessment for Learning' later in this chapter.

Teacher Tip

You don't have to be too ambitious when starting to use digital technologies in the Global Perspectives classroom, especially if this is something new to you. Make sure you keep the learning objective and success criteria in mind as you don't want the technology to become the focus of the lesson. If you are planning to use a digital technology that is new to you, follow the two-week rule:

Practise using the technology two weeks before you plan to use it with students to complete the activity.

This will give you a chance to sort out any problems and anticipate any questions that students might ask.

As well as making connections with others possible, digital technologies enable your students to work collaboratively with each other, for example by producing a presentation using software that allows each group member to edit it. You might try Google Docs or Prezi for this purpose.

▣ LESSON IDEA ONLINE 10.3: WORKING COLLABORATIVELY
Use this lesson idea as a way of getting students to work collaboratively.

In Chapter 9 **Inclusive education**, we explored the power of having choice. Using digital technologies also allows students more options. They can choose:

- how to complete a task
- who to work with
- where to work
- when to work
- what to produce.

How much choice students have depends on the parameters you set. You may want students to choose who to work with and what to produce by way of an outcome, such as a photo journal or a video clip. However, you might want them to work in class for the majority of the time, rather than at home whenever they feel like it. The amount of choice students have is also determined by the nature of the task. When completing a research report as a summative assessment, for example, you will set a deadline, but you can give students the choice of when and where to work to reach that deadline.

Teacher Tip

Using digital technologies in the Global Perspectives classroom helps to create global citizens, one of the aims of any Global Perspectives course. Here's how:

1 By helping students to access, identify, analyse and evaluate global mass media in different languages, including their first language and English. By doing this, students become

more aware of how and why different events, peoples, cultures and communities are represented by the global media. This can increase empathy and allow students to have a better understanding of the world they live in.

2 By widening students' experience of the opinions of others through digital media created by individuals, such as videos, blogs, podcasts, and so on. Try asking students to search for 'citizen journalist' reporters on the internet. These are individuals who often report on breaking news stories. Students can analyse the ways that these perspectives are similar and/or different from global media reports and why individual voices are important to a global conversation.

3 By encouraging students to join global knowledge networks. Rather than individual voices, these networks help students to realise the power of collective intelligence. There are many online collaborative science projects such as the GLOBE program (Global Learning and Observations to Benefit the Environment) run by NASA, where young people, educators and scientists collect and share information about global issues.

Using technology for effective teacher learning

As well as effective student learning, technology can be used for effective teacher learning. You might have considered connecting with other Global Perspectives teachers around the world. You and they are a source of information and ideas that can be shared easily via social media. Try searching for Global Perspectives teachers on Twitter. You could also follow Social Science, Humanities or Geography teachers as they might have ideas that you can use too.

Keeping yourself up to date about global topics, issues and places where you can source information is something else that digital technologies can help with. In fact, technology is an excellent way of accessing professional development as well as high-quality resources

My favourite five Twitter feeds for keeping up to date with what's going on around me are:

1 Global Citizen @GlblCtzn
2 BBC News (World) @ BBCWorld
3 TED Talks @TEDTalks

4   Guardian World @guardianworld
5   WWF (World Wildlife Fund) @WWF.

Teacher Tip

You might encourage students to use a social media platform to gather useful website links in one place. They can group them according to skill or topic, and access them quickly and easily just by going to the social media platform and logging in. When students come to produce their research report or team project, they can simply copy and paste their website addresses into their reference list, adding the names of the articles, the dates published and the dates they accessed the websites. You could do the same and share your links with other Global Perspectives teachers and your Global Perspectives students.

Two bookmarking websites to try are:

- Delicious
- Diigo.

One place to look for useful tips on using technology for teaching and learning is:

- Edutopia.

Using technology for Assessment for Learning

By using digital tools, you can more easily cater for all the individual needs in your Global Perspectives class. You can use the comments function in Word to give feedback about work to a student. The student can then act on the feedback by adding or amending in a different colour, for example.

Teacher Tip

Written feedback

When giving written feedback in Word, try having a conversation about work produced. Use phrases such as:

- I like the way you …
- Is there anything you might add here?

- I notice that you have …
- I wonder if you might …
- Do you mean …?
- What if you considered …?
- Might you have included …?

Audio feedback

As well as giving written feedback on students' work, you might have considered giving oral feedback by using the audio recording feature built into most smartphones. You might like to try it to provide personal and quality feedback to individual students.

You can give students the opportunity of taking on the role of the teacher to create and deliver their own Global Perspectives lesson, or you can ask students to find a source of information and create an activity around it. By providing these possibilities, your students will become more creative and learn in a more authentic way. As they are taking the lead in your lessons, you can then provide more one-to-one feedback as you will be moving around the classroom acting as a guide, giving you the opportunity to learn more about your students and their needs.

⊠ LESSON IDEA ONLINE 10.4: DESIGNING AND DELIVERING ACTIVITIES
Use this lesson idea to encourage students to design their own activities, to enable you to circulate and provide one-to-one feedback.

Another idea for using digital technologies for Assessment for Learning is to use live polling tools and quizzing tools. These can be used at the start or end of lessons to establish students' knowledge and understanding so that you know what to focus on to improve student performance. The information you gain from using these tools can help you identify the strengths and areas that individual students need to work on.

Three free digital tools to explore for Assessment for Learning are:

1 Kahoot
2 Google Forms
3 Quizlet.

Using technology for inclusive learning

As well as allowing students to choose the technology they use to complete a task, you can also provide them with differently graded resources such as templates, writing frames, images, and so on, to ensure that all students are able to achieve the set learning objective(s).

Templates and writing frames

Use templates and writing frames (as in Figure 8.2 in Chapter 8 **Language awareness**) to help students assimilate what they have learned and provide information. For example, when asking students to identify and explain information from spoken or written texts, get them to use a table like the one in Table 10.1. You can add a column entitled 'Other' for extra details that some students might pick out, but this can be an option rather than a requirement.

	Perspective	Issue	Cause	Consequence	Other
1					
2					
3					

Table 10.1: Gathering information from a text.

Internet sources

In Chapter 9 **Inclusive education**, we explored the idea of students having multiple intelligences. You might, therefore, give students a range of internet sources about the same issue, but with different levels of challenge. They can then choose a source or a couple of sources they are most comfortable with, for example, texts of different lengths and complexity, images, podcasts, video clips and blogs.

Images

Images are a great way of ensuring that everyone can access the content of a text. Provide a larger range of images to support those students that need them and fewer for those that need extra challenge. Ask students to source their own images to add to a text. This will give you a good idea of the level of understanding, and encourage students to do their own research.

Graphic organisers

Graphic organisers were mentioned in Chapter 5 **Active learning** as a way of helping students organise their thoughts and ideas. There are many online tools that can replace paper-based graphic organisers, like the KWL chart used in Lesson idea 5.3. Try a mind-mapping tool. Students can add words, phrases, questions and visuals.

Mind maps:

- record what students already know about a topic or issue, connecting prior learning to new learning
- allow students to add words and images connected to the central idea or issue, or any branches off the central idea
- aid memory because of the layout of the images and phrases, especially if you ask students to provide a commentary with their mind map.

Support written work with verbal commentaries

When giving students a written text, you can also record it and play it as students read or enable students to have access to the recording and headphones. You might add extra information or explain words or phrases in the commentary. Students can play the recording as they read. They can pause it as often as they need to, perhaps to look up words in their dictionary or to make notes, and replay sections as necessary.

Summary

In this chapter, we have focused on using technology for teaching and learning in Global Perspectives lessons.

Remember:

- Technology is a tool. As such, it should be used to enable students to meet a set learning objective. If using a digital technology for the first time, follow the two-week rule.

- The use of digital technologies for student learning encourages students to identify, analyse and evaluate a wide range of perspectives from a wide variety of media.

- Digital technologies are a great way of giving feedback and personalising learning, thereby encouraging student progression and making your Global Perspectives lessons more inclusive.

11 | Global thinking

What is global thinking?

Global thinking is about learning how to live in a complex world as an active and engaged citizen. It is about considering the bigger picture and appreciating the nature and depth of our shared humanity.

When we encourage global thinking in students we help them recognise, examine and express their own and others' perspectives. We need to scaffold students' thinking to enable them to engage on cognitive, social and emotional levels, and construct their understanding of the world to be able to participate fully in its future.

We as teachers can help students develop routines and habits of mind to enable them to move beyond the familiar, discern that which is of local and global significance, make comparisons, take a cultural perspective and challenge stereotypes. We can encourage them to learn about contexts and traditions, and provide opportunities for them to reflect on their own and others' viewpoints.

Why adopt a global thinking approach?

Global thinking is particularly relevant in an interconnected, digitised world where ideas, opinions and trends are rapidly and relentlessly circulated. Students learn to pause and evaluate. They study why a topic is important on a personal, local and global scale, and they will be motivated to understand the world and their significance in it. Students gain a deeper understanding of why different viewpoints and ideas are held across the world.

Global thinking is something we can nurture both within and across disciplines. We can invite students to learn how to use different lenses from each discipline to see and interpret the world. They also learn how best to apply and communicate key concepts within and across disciplines. We can help our students select the appropriate media and technology to communicate and create their own personal synthesis of the information they have gathered.

Global thinking enables students to become more rounded individuals who perceive themselves as actors in a global context and who value diversity. It encourages them to become more aware, curious and interested in learning about the world and how it works. It helps students to challenge assumptions and stereotypes, to be better informed and more respectful. Global thinking takes the focus beyond exams and grades, or even checklists of skills and attributes. It develops students who are more ready to compete in the global marketplace and more able to participate effectively in an interconnected world.

What are the challenges of incorporating global thinking?

The pressures of an already full curriculum, the need to meet national and local standards, and the demands of exam preparation may make it seem challenging to find time to incorporate global thinking into lessons and programmes of study. A whole-school approach may be required for global thinking to be incorporated in subject plans for teaching and learning.

We need to give all students the opportunity to find their voice and participate actively and confidently, regardless of their background and world experiences, when exploring issues of global significance. We need to design suitable activities that are clear, ongoing and varying. Students need to be able to connect with materials, and extend and challenge their thinking. We also need to devise and use new forms of assessment that incorporate flexible and cooperative thinking.

Global Perspectives is about global thinking

Global Perspectives as a course of study is about getting students to think more globally. It's about looking at local issues that have global significance, and understanding and appreciating different perspectives. It's also about thinking globally and acting locally.

> ☑ **LESSON IDEA ONLINE 11.1: THINK GLOBALLY, ACT LOCALLY**
> Use this lesson idea as a way of exploring what it means to think globally and act locally.

The learning objectives you set for students to meet the Global Perspectives assessment objectives – research, analysis, evaluation, reflection, communication and collaboration – will allow them to recognise, examine and express not only their own but also others' perspectives, as we explored in Chapter 3 **The nature of the subject and key considerations**. In your Global Perspectives lessons, students learn how to be active and engaged citizens.

This chapter about global thinking complements the rest of the chapters in this book in that it investigates further ways of encouraging your students to be active global citizens, to be entrepreneurial and collaborative, and to be prepared for the world of further study and work.

Creating active global citizens

Active global citizens consider the impact that their actions has on others, as explored in Lesson idea 11.1. A great example I use is to ask students to consider how much water they use in a single day. You can get them to make a list with a partner. On their list, they are likely to have uses such as bathing, showering, washing teeth, washing pots and clothes, and so on. Then ask them to think of any other uses of water – extending this beyond the personal to the national and the global; for example, swimming pools, golf courses, watering plants, and so on. This leads nicely into a research activity to find out how much water an average person in one country uses compared to someone in a different part of the world.

To make students aware of similarities and differences in behaviour, try to relate examples to their own lives. The use of water already mentioned is a good example. You might also focus on how much electricity a family in the developed world uses, or how much money a family spends on fast food or fizzy soft drinks. Once you have explored the similarities and differences, both within your Global Perspectives class and by asking students to do research, you can ask students to think about how they can take action as active global citizens, both individually and collectively. One form of individual action might be to reduce the amount of water used, for example by having a shower instead of a bath, or by reusing towels when on holiday in a hotel rather than having them washed every day. Holding a fund-raising event (e.g. selling cakes) for a charity such as WaterAid is an example of collective action.

Asking questions can help create active global citizens and persuade students of the importance of not making assumptions, but, rather, using evidence gathered from their research. Encourage students to ask the following questions:

- Where can I find information to help me better understand what is happening in the world and how this relates to my community?
- What issues are happening around the world, and how do they affect my community?
- What local organisations exist that are helping with global issues of concern?

☑ LESSON IDEA ONLINE 11.2: IDENTIFYING GLOBAL ISSUES
Use this lesson idea as a way of getting students to think about their responses.

Primary research

Students can do some primary research to find out about the issues concerning people in their community. Students could give out a questionnaire to friends, family and local people they know. They could limit numbers to ten to start with. This will give them an overview of the issues that are important to people and the reasons for this importance.

You will need to help students decide on the research methods they are going to use, depending on the sort of data that they want to collect: numerical data, which might indicate how many people think that something is an important local issue, and/or narrative data, to explain why they think this. Both numerical and narrative data can be gathered by way of a questionnaire, but students might also want to conduct some short interviews.

Teacher Tip

When interviewing people, it's important that students behave in a way that keeps the respondents they are interviewing from harm, and that they treat all the information gained confidentially. There is no need for them to mention names once they have their research findings. They can simply explain that they did some primary research and how the findings from this research helped them to decide on their issue.

☑ LESSON IDEA ONLINE 11.3: UNDERTAKING PRIMARY RESEARCH

Use this lesson idea as a starter activity for students to reflect on the process of undertaking primary research.

Local organisations

One way of finding out about local organisations that exist to help identify and investigate issues is for students to look in local newsletters, newspapers and community publications. Public places like supermarkets and libraries often have leaflets advertising local organisations. Youth groups are another source of local information, as is the school and other schools within the community. It is likely that, during your Global Perspectives course, students will want to do something in their school as a way of taking action.

Teacher Tip

Taking action is an excellent way of encouraging students to respond to their research about a local issue with global significance. However, students are taking action just as effectively if they present their research findings to an audience of peers or younger students in school as if they were to volunteer at a local wildlife park on a Saturday. The first option might even be more effective if, for example, students have collaborated as a team and produced a drama sketch as a way of raising awareness about an issue.

Being entrepreneurial

Part of being entrepreneurial is being able and willing to take action. Entrepreneurs also take risks for something they are passionate about. They are open to different possibilities and they strive to make improvements. Global Perspectives teaches students to be entrepreneurial by promoting collaboration in teams as well as undertaking individual study and work.

Entrepreneurs are often creative in that they reflect on different ways of making a difference. They are also usually good at problem-solving. This might be related to business and finance, but it doesn't have to be. Try asking your students whether they can think of any entrepreneurs and what made them entrepreneurs. Some of the people they come up with might be naturally more creative and better at solving problems than others. For many, however, creativity and problem-solving skills can be developed just like any other skill. Global Perspectives provides the perfect forum for developing creativity and problem-solving skills. Here are just three ways to do this:

1 Teams work together to discuss ways of resolving issues they are interested in.
2 Teams can produce all number of creative outcomes to raise awareness about issues, such as posters, poems, songs, lessons, cartoons and video clips.
3 Individuals explore different perspectives of an issue and the causes and consequences of the issue, in an attempt to formulate courses of action to help resolve or improve the issue.

☑ **LESSON IDEA ONLINE 11.4: DEVELOPING CREATIVITY**
Use this lesson idea as a way of getting students to think more creatively to plan a research report or a team project.

Problem-solving

When trying to solve a problem, students might find the questions in Figure 11.1 useful.

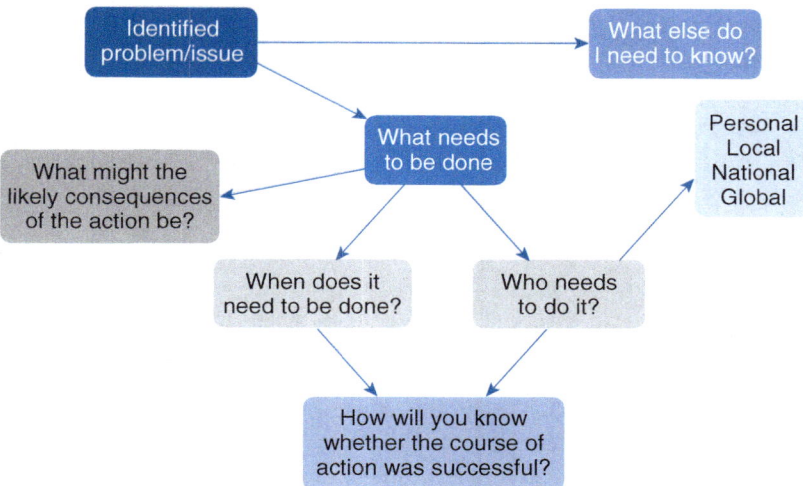

Figure 11.1: Questions for problem-solving.

Working collaboratively

Collaboration is a large part of any Global Perspectives course. Its importance is emphasised by the fact that it is an assessment objective and, as such, there is a summative assessment that involves collaboration.

Teacher Tip

Each Global Perspectives syllabus requires students to collaborate. Sometimes students will be working together to plan, research, discuss and produce something, for example a presentation, a video clip, a drama sketch, or a website page. Afterwards, they write a reflective paper on their own. At other times, they will be planning, researching and discussing as a team, to then produce something individually, for example a presentation, as well as writing an individual reflective paper. Therefore, it is vitally important that we give students opportunities to work collaboratively from the beginning of their Global Perspectives course.

☑ **LESSON IDEA ONLINE 11.5: WORKING COLLABORATIVELY**
Use this lesson idea to encourage collaboration. It can be used for any global topic or issue.

Team roles

We cannot always assume that students know how to work collaboratively in teams, although they may already be doing so in your lessons. With enough practice they will automatically start planning and deciding on roles and responsibilities, but before they get to this stage, we need to guide students when setting up collaborative projects.

According to industrial psychologist David Merrill, the roles we take on in teams depend very much on the way we like to work, known as 'work styles'. Merrill categorises these work styles into four distinct groups:

1 *Drivers* seek control and are people who like to take charge, making them ideal leaders of teams.
2 *Expressive people* are creative. They interact well with others and are willing to share their ideas, feelings and opinions. These characteristics made them good at encouraging others to arrive at decisions.
3 *Amiable people* are good at teamwork and listening. They prefer to be told what to do than to lead. They make very good recorders in that they are good at keeping notes of the discussions taking place within the team.
4 *Analytical people* like organisation and structure, and generally prefer to work alone rather than in teams. They make good checkers as they keep track of what everyone is doing and try to ensure that deadlines are met.

This is just a short summary of the characteristics for each work style. Further information can be found by searching on the internet for 'David Merrill' and 'work styles'. You can probably already identify the work styles of your students so might want to use this information to form teams. You might like to spend some time asking students to identify their own work and each other's work styles. This will get students thinking about their strengths and weaknesses, and the role they might play when working collaboratively.

Empathy

To truly understand the interdependence between people, the environment, and the consequences of personal, local, national and global actions, we need empathy. Students often watch documentary films that might shock them or they may feel sorry for the people in them, but as it's not directly affecting them, they soon forget. To develop empathy, we need to provide opportunities for students to 'walk in someone else's shoes'.

Six great discussion questions focusing on empathy

1 What is empathy, and how does it differ from sympathy?
2 What does it mean to say 'don't criticise someone until you've walked a mile in their shoes'?
3 Why do you think some people find it easier to empathise than others?
4 Why do you think it might be hard to show empathy?
5 How can we show more empathy towards other people?
6 Mother Teresa spent most of her life helping the poorest, sickest people of Kolkata, India. She once said: 'I want you to be concerned with your next-door neighbour. Do you know your next-door neighbour?' How does this quotation relate to empathy?

Figure 11.2 gives five steps to use to develop students' ability to empathise.

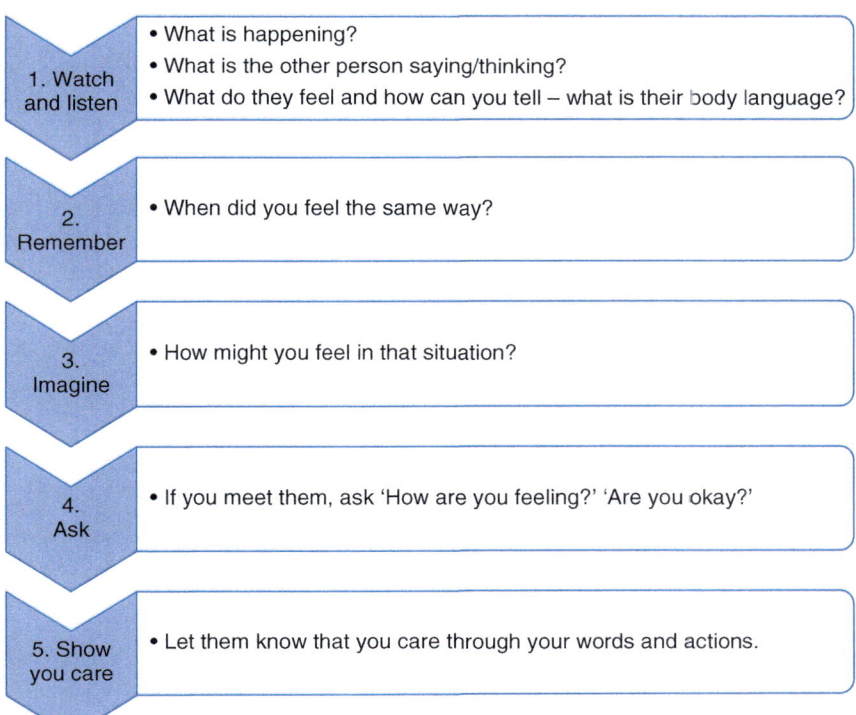

Figure 11.2: Five steps to develop empathy.

☑ **LESSON IDEA ONLINE 11.6: DEVELOPING EMPATHY**

Use this lesson idea to develop your students' ability to empathise. You can use images from any global topic or issue.

Assessment and feedback

Global thinking also requires us as teachers to think globally. One way of doing this is to incorporate a focus on global thinking into assessment and feedback. This can be done by you or by your students themselves when they peer and self-assess, as you saw in Lesson idea 11.5.

☑ **LESSON IDEA ONLINE 11.7: ASSESSING COLLABORATIVE PROJECTS**

Use this lesson idea as a way of assessing and providing feedback on a collaborative project. You can find further ideas in Chapter 6 **Assessment for Learning**.

Preparing for further study and the world of work

Global Perspectives prepares students for further study and the world of work by enabling them to collaborate on different projects, and to work independently: undertaking research, and deconstructing and reconstructing arguments. When deconstructing arguments, students:

- identify and critically compare different perspectives
- differentiate between fact, opinion, value judgement, prediction, explanation, bias and vested interest
- identify the key components of a claim or an argument, such as conclusions, assumptions, reasoning and evidence
- evaluate the strengths and weaknesses within arguments, reasoning and claims.

Teacher Tip

When deconstructing an argument, students might ask themselves the following six questions:

1 Is this an argument or a report, and does it contain facts, opinions, predictions, value judgements, bias, vested interest or a mixture of these?
2 What is the author trying to convince us to believe or accept? Has the author stated this conclusion or is it only implied?
3 Why is the author trying to persuade us to accept the conclusion(s)?
4 What else do I need to know or be persuaded of in order to accept the conclusion(s)?
5 What evidence does the author use to support their reasoning?
6 How convincing is the reasoning in the argument?

Being able to formulate an argument

When formulating their own argument, students use the evidence that they have found during the deconstruction phase. They may have deconstructed a local or a national argument about an issue, for example, whether it's right to continue to burn fossil fuels for economic development. They then research the evidence for different perspectives. This ensures that they have looked at the issue from a global as well as a local or a national perspective. In their argument, they compare causes and consequences of the identified issue, evaluating their sources of evidence for reliability and credibility, before proposing courses of action to help resolve or improve the issue. Finally, they conclude by reflecting on the issue and how their perspective might have changed as a result of their research findings and the evidence they have found. Figure 11.3 gives a visual of the things to consider when developing an argument, and can be used to help your students structure their arguments effectively.

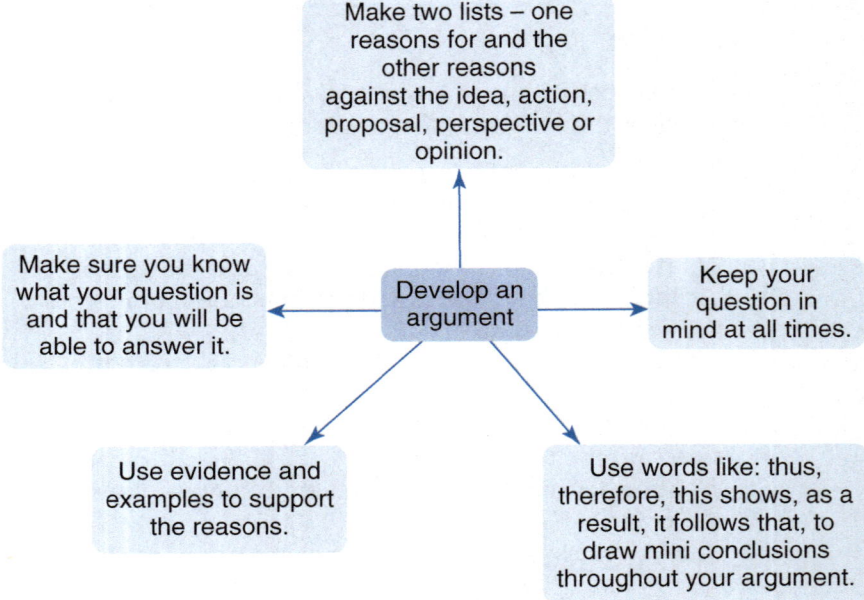

Figure 11.3: Developing an argument.

☑ LESSON IDEA ONLINE 11.8: DEVELOPING AN ARGUMENT

Use this lesson idea as a way of getting students to develop their own arguments.

You can support students when they develop arguments by providing some connectives and sentence starters. Here's a list you might want to give to your students. See Chapter 8 **Language awareness** and Chapter 9 **Inclusive education** for further ideas to support students' learning in Global Perspectives.

Some people believe that …	However, others think that …	Supporters argue that …
There is no doubt that …	It is claimed that …	However, it could be argued that …
_____ is/are a particular problem because …	An additional problem is …	Furthermore …
Consequently …	Therefore …	On one hand …
An opposing perspective might be …	On the contrary …	On the other hand …

Would ...?	Is it right to ...?	Do you agree that ...?
For example ...	This fact ...	For instance ...
As well as ...	Moreover ...	Additionally ...
In conclusion ...	To conclude ...	As a result ..

Summary

In this chapter, we have explored what global thinking is and how Global Perspectives promotes global thinking.

Remember:

- Global thinking is about understanding and appreciating different perspectives so that each student can become an active and engaged global citizen during their time at school and beyond.

- Global Perspectives requires students to think about global issues of concern and how they connect locally and personally so that they can take action both individually and collectively.

- Global Perspectives develops all the skills necessary to be a global thinker. As global thinkers, students are more aware of the world around them. They challenge assumptions and stereotypes. They are more persuasive in arguments, and they are better informed to make decisions now and in the future. Ask yourself: Are my students global thinkers?

12 Reflective practice

Dr Paul Beedle, Head of Professional Development
Qualifications, Cambridge International Examinations

'As a teacher you are always learning'

It is easy to say this, isn't it? Is it true? Are you bound to learn just by being a teacher?

You can learn every day from the experience of working with your students, collaborating with your colleagues and playing your part in the life of your school. You can learn also by being receptive to new ideas and approaches, and by applying and evaluating these in practice in your own context.

To be more precise, let us say that as a teacher:

- You **should** always be learning
  to develop your expertise throughout your career for your own fulfilment as a member of the teaching profession and to be as effective as possible in the classroom.
- You **can** always be learning
  if you approach the teaching experience with an open mind, ready to learn and knowing how to reflect on what you are doing in order to improve.

You want your professional development activities to be as relevant as possible to what you do and who you are, and to help change the quality of your teaching and your students' learning – for the better, in terms of outcomes, and for good, in terms of lasting effect. You want to feel that 'it all makes sense' and that you are actively following a path that works for you personally, professionally and career-wise.

So professional learning is about making the most of opportunities and your working environment, bearing in mind who you are, what you are like and how you want to improve. But simply experiencing – thinking about and responding to situations, and absorbing ideas and information – is not necessarily learning. It is through reflection that you can make the most of your experience to deepen and extend your professional skills and understanding.

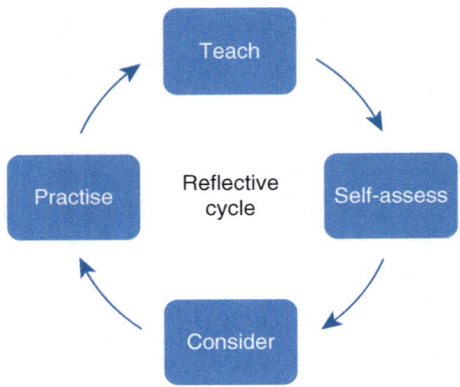

Figure 12.1

In this chapter, we will focus on three *essentials* of reflective practice, explaining in principle and in practice how you can support your own continuing professional development:

1 **Focusing** on what you want to learn about and why
2 **Challenging** yourself and others to go beyond description and assumptions to critical analysis and evaluation
3 **Sharing** what you are learning with colleagues – to enrich understanding and enhance the quality of practice.

These essentials will help you as you apply and adapt the rich ideas and approaches in this book in your own particular context. They will also help you if you are, or are about to be, taking part in a Cambridge Professional Development Qualification (Cambridge PDQ) programme, to make the most of your programme, develop your portfolio and gain the qualification.

1   Focus
In principle

Given the multiple dimensions and demands of being a teacher, you might be tempted to try to cover 'everything' in your professional development but you will then not have the time to go beneath the surface much at all. Likewise, attending many different training events will certainly keep you very busy but it is unlikely that these will simply add up to improving your thinking and practice in sustainable and systematic ways.

Teachers who are beginning an organised programme of professional learning find that it is most helpful to select particular ideas, approaches and topics which are relevant to their own situation and their school's priorities. They can then be clear about their professional learning goals, and how their own learning contributes to improving their students' learning outcomes. They deliberately choose activities that help make sense of their practice with their students in their school and have clear overall purpose.

It is one thing achieving focus, and another maintaining this over time. When the going gets tough, because it is difficult either to understand or become familiar with new ideas and practices, or to balance learning time with the demands of work and life, it really helps to have a mission – to know why you want to learn something as well as what that something is. Make sure that this is a purpose which you feel genuinely belongs to you and in which you have a keen interest, rather than it being something given to you or imposed on you. Articulate your focus not just by writing it down but by 'pitching' it to a colleague whose opinion you trust and taking note of their feedback.

In practice

- Plan
  What is my goal and how will I approach the activity?

  Select an approach that is new to you, but make sure that you understand the thinking behind this and that it is relevant to your students' learning. Do it for real effect, not for show.

- Monitor
  Am I making progress towards my goal; do I need to try a different approach?

  Take time during your professional development programme to review how far and well you are developing your understanding of theory and practice. What can you do to get more out of the experience, for example by discussing issues with your mentor, researching particular points, and asking your colleagues for their advice?

- Evaluate
  What went well, what could have been better, what have I learned for next time?

  Evaluation can sometimes be seen as a 'duty to perform' – like clearing up after the event – rather than the pivotal moment in learning that it really is. Evaluate not because you are told you have to; evaluate to make sense of the learning experience you have been through and what it means to you, and to plan ahead to see what you can do in the future.

This cycle of planning, monitoring and evaluation is just as relevant to you as a professional learner as to your students as learners. Be actively in charge of your learning and take appropriate actions. Make your professional development work for you. Of course your professional development programme leaders, trainers and mentors will guide and support you in your learning, but you are at the heart of your own learning experience, not on the receiving end of something that is cast in stone. Those who assist and advise you on your professional development want you and your colleagues to get the best out of the experience, and need your feedback along the way so that if necessary they can adapt and improve what they are devising.

2 Challenge
In principle

Reflection is a constructive process that helps the individual teacher to improve their thinking and practice. It involves regularly asking questions of yourself about your developing ideas and experience, and keeping track of your developing thinking, for example in a reflective journal. Reflection is continuous, rather than a one-off experience. Being honest with yourself means thinking hard, prompting yourself to go beyond your first thoughts about a new experience and to avoid taking for granted your opinions about something to which you are accustomed. Be a critical friend to yourself.

In the Cambridge PDQ Certificate in Teaching and Learning, for example, teachers take a fresh look at the concepts and processes of learning and challenge their own assumptions. They engage with theory and models of effective teaching and learning, and open their minds through observing experienced practitioners, applying new ideas in practice and listening to formative feedback from mentors and colleagues. To evidence in their assessed portfolio how they have learned from this experience, they not only present records of observed practice but also critical analysis showing understanding of how and why practices work and how they can be put into different contexts successfully.

The Cambridge PDQ syllabuses set out key questions to focus professional learning and the portfolio templates prompts to help you. These questions provide a framework for reflection. They are open-ended and will not only stimulate your thinking but lead to lively group discussion. The discipline of asking yourself and others questions such as 'Why?' 'How do we know?' 'What is the evidence?' 'What are the conditions?' leads to thoughtful and intelligent practice.

In practice

Challenge:

- Yourself, as you reflect on an experience, to be more critical in your thinking. For example, rather than simply describing what happened, analyse why it happened and its significance, and what might have happened if conditions had been different.
- Theory – by understanding and analysing the argument, and evaluating the evidence that supports the theory. Don't simply accept a theory as a given fact – be sure that you feel that the ideas make sense and that there is positive value in applying them in practice.
- Convention – the concept of 'best practice(s)' is as good as we know now, on the basis of the body of evidence, for example on the effect size of impact of a particular approach on learning outcomes. By using an approach in an informed way and with a critical eye, you can evaluate the approach relating to your particular situation.

3 Share

In principle

Schools are such busy places, and yet teachers can feel they are working on their own for long periods because of the intensity of their workload as they focus on all that is involved in teaching their students. We know that a crucial part of our students' active learning is the opportunity to collaborate with their peers in order to investigate, create and communicate. Just so with professional learning: teachers learn best through engagement with their peers, in their own school and beyond. Discussion and interaction with colleagues, focused on learning and student outcomes, and carried out in a culture of openness, trust and respect, helps each member of the community of practice in the school clarify and sharpen their understanding and enhance their practice.

This is why the best professional learning programmes incorporate collaborative learning, and pivotal moments are designed into the programme for this to happen frequently over time: formally in guided learning sessions such as workshops and more informally in opportunities such as study group, teach meets and discussion, both face-to-face and online.

In practice

Go beyond expectations!

In the Cambridge PDQ syllabus, each candidate needs to carry out an observation of an experienced practitioner and to be observed formatively themselves by their mentor on a small number of occasions. This is the formal requirement in terms of evidence of practice within the portfolio for the qualification. The expectation is that these are not the only times that teachers will observe and be observed for professional learning purposes (rather than performance appraisal).

However, the more that teachers can observe each other's teaching, the better; sharing of practice leads to advancement of shared knowledge and understanding of aspects of teaching and learning, and development of agreed shared 'best practice'.

So:

- open your classroom door to observation
- share with your closest colleague(s) when you are trying out a fresh approach, for example an idea in this book
- ask them to look for particular aspects in the lesson, especially how students are engaging with the approach – pose an observation question
- reflect with them after the lesson on what you and they have learned from the experience – pose an evaluation question
- go and observe them as they do the same
- after a number of lessons, discuss with your colleagues how you can build on your peer observation with common purpose, for example lesson study
- share with your other colleagues in the school what you are gaining from this collaboration and encourage them to do the same
- always have question(s) to focus observations and focus these question(s) on student outcomes.

Pathways

The short-term effects of professional development are very much centred on teachers' students. For example, the professional learning in a Cambridge PDQ programme should lead directly and quickly to changes in the ways your students learn. All teachers have this at heart – the desire to help their students learn better.

The long-term effects of professional development are more teacher-centric. During their career over, say, 30 years, a teacher may teach many thousand lessons. There are many good reasons for a teacher to keep up-to-date with pedagogy, not least to sustain their enjoyment of what they do.

Each teacher will follow their own career pathway, taking into account many factors. We do work within systems, at school and wider level, involving salary and appointment levels, and professional development can be linked to these as requirement or expectation. However, to a significant extent teachers shape their own career pathway, making decisions along the way. Their pathway is not pre-ordained; there is room for personal choice, opportunity and serendipity. It is for each teacher to judge for themselves how much they wish to venture. A teacher's professional development pathway should reflect and support this.

It is a big decision to embark on an extended programme of professional development, involving a significant commitment of hours of learning and preparation over several months. You need to be as clear as you can be about the immediate and long-term value of such a commitment. Will your programme lead to academic credit as part of a stepped pathway towards Masters level, for example?

Throughout your career, you need to be mindful of the opportunities you have for professional development. Gauge the value of options available at each particular stage in your professional life, both in terms of relevance to your current situation – your students, subject and phase focus, and school – and the future situation(s) of which you are thinking.

13

Understanding the impact of classroom practice on student progress

Lee Davis, Deputy Director for Education, Cambridge International Examinations

Introduction

Throughout this book, you have been encouraged to adopt a more active approach to teaching and learning and to ensure that formative assessment is embedded into your classroom practice. In addition, you have been asked to develop your students as meta-learners, such that they are able to, as the academic Chris Watkins puts it, 'narrate their own learning' and become more reflective and strategic in how they plan, carry out and then review any given learning activity.

A key question remains, however. How will you know that the new strategies and approaches you intend to adopt have made a significant difference to your students' progress and learning? What, in other words, has been the impact and how will you know?

This chapter looks at how you might go about determining this at the classroom level. It deliberately avoids reference to whole-school student tracking systems, because these are not readily available to all schools and all teachers. Instead, it considers what you can do as an individual teacher to make the learning of your students visible – both to you and anyone else who is interested in how they are doing. It does so by introducing the concept of 'effect sizes' and shows how these can be used by teachers to determine not just whether an intervention works or not but, more importantly, *how well* it works. 'Effect size' is a useful way of quantifying or measuring the size of any difference between two groups or data sets. The aim is to place emphasis on the most important aspect of an intervention or change in teaching approach – the **size of the effect** on student outcomes.

Consider the following scenario:

Over the course of a term, a teacher has worked hard with her students on understanding 'what success looks like' for any given task or activity. She has stressed the importance of everyone being clear about the criteria for success, before students embark upon the chosen task and plan their way through it. She has even got to the point where students have been co-authors of the assessment rubrics used, so that they have been fully engaged in the intended outcomes throughout and can articulate what is required before they have even started. The teacher is happy with developments so far, but has it made a difference to student progress? Has learning increased beyond what we would normally expect for an average student over a term anyway?

Here is an extract from the teacher's markbook.

Student	Sept Task	Nov Task
Katya	13	15
Maria	15	20
Joao	17	23
David	20	18
Mushtaq	23	25
Caio	25	38
Cristina	28	42
Tom	30	35
Hema	32	37
Jennifer	35	40

Figure 14.1

Before we start analysing this data, we must note the following:

- The task given in September was at the start of the term – the task in November was towards the end of the term.
- Both tasks assessed similar skills, knowledge and understanding in the student.
- The maximum mark for each was 50.
- The only variable that has changed over the course of the term is the approaches to teaching and learning by the teacher. All other things are equal.

With that in mind, looking at Figure 14.1, what conclusions might you draw as an external observer?

You might be saying something along the lines of: 'Mushtaq and Katya have made some progress, but not very much. Caio and Cristina appear to have done particularly well. David, on the other hand, appears to be going backwards!'

What can you say about the class as a whole?

Calculating effect sizes

What if we were to apply the concept of 'effect sizes' to the class results in Figure 14.1, so that we could make some more definitive statements about the impact of the interventions over the given time period? Remember, we are doing so in order to understand the size of the effect on student outcomes or progress.

Let's start by understanding how it is calculated.

An effect size is found by calculating 'the standardised mean difference between two data sets or groups'. In essence, this means we are looking for the difference between two averages, while taking into the account the spread of values (in this case, marks) around those averages at the same time.

As a formula, and from Figure 14.1, it looks like the following:

$$\text{Effect size} = \frac{\text{average class mark (after intervention)} - \text{average class mark (before intervention)}}{\text{spread (standard deviation of the class)}}$$

In words: the average mark achieved by the class *before* the teacher introduced her intervention strategies is taken away from the average mark achieved by the class *after* the intervention strategies. This is then divided by the standard deviation[1] of the class as a whole.

---

[1] The standard deviation is merely a way of expressing by how much the members of a group (in this case, student marks in the class) differ from the average value (or mark) for the group.

Inserting our data into a spreadsheet helps us calculate the effect size as follows:

	A	B	C
1	**Student**	September Task	November Task
2	Katya	13	15
3	Maria	15	20
4	Joao	17	23
5	David	20	18
6	Mushtaq	23	25
7	Caio	25	38
8	Cristina	28	42
9	Tom	30	35
10	Hema	32	37
11	Jennifer	35	40
12			
13	Average mark	23.8 = AVERAGE (B2:B11)	29.3 = AVERAGE (C2:C11)
14	Standard deviation	7.5 = STDEV (B2:B11)	10.11 = STDEV (C2:C11)

Figure 14.2

Therefore, the effect size for this class $= \dfrac{29.3 - 23.8}{8.8} = 0.62$
But what does this mean?

Interpreting effect sizes for classroom practice

In pure statistical terms, a 0.62 effect size means that the average student mark **after** the intervention by the teacher, is 0.62 standard deviations above the average student mark **before** the intervention.

We can state this in another way: the post-intervention average mark now exceeds 61% of the student marks previously.

Going further, we can also say that the average student mark, post-intervention, would have placed a student in the top four in the class previously. You can see this visually in Figure 14.2 where 29.3 (the class average after the teacher's interventions) would have been between Cristina's and Tom's marks in the September task.

This is good, isn't it? As a teacher, would you be happy with this progress by the class over the term?

To help understand effect sizes further, and therefore how well or otherwise the teacher has done above, let us look at how they are used in large-scale studies as well as research into educational effectiveness more broadly. We will then turn our attention to what really matters – talking about student learning.

Effect sizes in research

We know from results analyses of the Program for International Student Assessment (PISA) and the Trends in International Mathematics and Science Study (TIMMS) that, across the world, a year's schooling leads to an effect size of 0.4. John Hattie and his team at The University of Melbourne reached similar conclusions when looking at over 900 meta-analyses of classroom and whole-school interventions to improve student learning – 240 million students later, the result was an effect size of 0.4 on average for all these strategies.

What this means, then, is that any teacher achieving an effect size of greater than 0.4 is doing better than expected (than the average) over the course of a year. From our example above, not only are the students making better than expected progress, they are also doing so in just one term.

Here is something else to consider. In England, the distribution of GCSE grades in Maths and English have standard deviations of between 1.5 and 1.8 grades (A★, A, B, C, etc.), so an improvement of one GCSE grade represents an effect size of between 0.5 and 0.7. This means that, in the context of secondary schools, introducing a change in classroom practice of 0.62 (as the teacher achieved above) would result in an improvement of about one GCSE grade for each student in the subject.

Furthermore, for a school in which 50% of students were previously attaining five or more A★–C grades, this percentage (assuming the effect size of 0.62 applied equally across all subjects and all other things being equal) the percentage would rise to 73%.

Now, that's something worth knowing.

What next for your classroom practice? Talking about student learning

Given what we now know about effect sizes, what might be the practical next steps for you as a teacher?

Firstly, try calculating effect sizes for yourself, using marks and scores for your students that are comparable, e.g. student performance on key skills in maths, reading, writing, science practicals, etc. Become familiar with how they are calculated so that you can then start interrogating them 'intelligently'.

Do the results indicate progress was made? If so, how much is attributable to the interventions you have introduced?

Try calculating effect sizes for each individual student, in addition to your class, to make their progress visible too. To help illustrate this, let us return to the comments we were making about the progress of some students in Figure 14.1. We thought Cristina and Caio did very well and we had grave concerns about David. Individual effect sizes for the class of students would help us shed light on this further:

Student	September Task	November task	Individual Effect Size
Katya	13	15	0.22*
Maria	15	20	0.55
Joao	17	23	0.66
David	20	18	-0.22
Mushtaq	23	25	0.22
Caio	25	38	1.43
Cristina	28	42	1.54
Tom	30	35	0.55
Hema	32	37	0.55
Jennifer	35	40	0.55

* The individual effect size for each student above is calculated by taking their September mark away from their November mark and then dividing by the standard deviation for the class – in this case 8.8.

Figure 14.3

If these were your students, what questions would you now ask of yourself, of your students and even of your colleagues, to help you understand why the results are as they are and how learning is best achieved? Remember, an effect size of 0.4 is our benchmark, so who is doing better than that? Who is not making the progress we would expect?

David's situation immediately stands out, doesn't it? A negative effect size implies learning has regressed. So, what has happened, and how will we draw alongside him to find out what the issues are and how best to address them?

Why did Caio and Cristina do so well, considering they were just above average previously? Effect sizes of 1.43 and 1.54 respectively are significantly above the benchmark, so what has changed from their perspective? Perhaps they responded particularly positively to developing assessment rubrics together. Perhaps learning had sometimes been a mystery to them before, but with success criteria now made clear, this obstacle to learning had been removed.

We don't know the answers to these questions, but they would be great to ask, wouldn't they? So go ahead and ask them. Engage in dialogue with your students, and see how their own ability to discuss their learning has changed and developed. This will be as powerful a way as any of discovering whether your new approaches to teaching and learning have had an impact and it ultimately puts data, such as effect sizes, into context.

Concluding remarks

Effect sizes are a very effective means of helping you understand the impact of your classroom practice upon student progress. If you change your teaching strategies in some way, calculating effect sizes, for both the class and each individual student, helps you determine not just *if* learning has improved, but by *how much*.

They are, though, only part of the process. As teachers, we must look at the data carefully and intelligently in order to understand 'why'. Why did some students do better than others? Why did some not make any progress at all? Use effect sizes as a starting point, not the end in itself.

Ensure that you don't do this in isolation – collaborate with others and share this approach with them. What are your colleagues finding in their classes, in their subjects? Are the same students making the same progress across the curriculum? If there are differences, what might account for them?

In answering such questions, we will be in a much better position to determine next steps in the learning process for students. After all, isn't that our primary purpose as teachers?

Acknowledgements, further reading and resources

This chapter has drawn extensively on the influential work of the academics John Hattie and Robert Coe. You are encouraged to look at the following resources to develop your understanding further:

Hattie, J. (2012). *Visible Learning for Teachers – Maximising Impact on Learning*. London and New York: Routledge.

Coe, R. (2002). *It's the Effect Size, Stupid. What effect size is and why it is important.* Paper presented at the Annual Conference of The British Educational Research Association, University of Exeter, England, 12–14 September, 2002. A version of the paper is available online on the University of Leeds website.

The Centre for Evaluation and Monitoring, University of Durham, has produced a very useful effect size calculator (available from their website). Note that it also calculates a confidence interval for any effect size generated. Confidence intervals are useful in helping you understand the margin for error of an effect size you are reporting for your class. These are particularly important when the sample size is small, which will inevitably be the case for most classroom teachers.

14 Recommended reading

For a deeper understanding of the Cambridge approach, refer to the Cambridge International Examinations website (www. cie.org.uk/teaching-and-learning) where you will find the following in-depth guides:

Implementing the curriculum with Cambridge; a guide for school leaders.

Developing your school with Cambridge; a guide for school leaders.

Education briefs for a number of topics, such as active learning and bilingual education. Each brief includes information about the challenges and benefits of different approaches to teaching, practical tips, lists of resources.

Getting started with… These are interactive resources to help to explore and develop areas of teaching and learning. They include practical examples, reflective questions, and experiences from teachers and researchers.

For further support around becoming a Cambridge school visit cambridge-community.org.uk.

The resources in this section can be used as a supplement to your learning, to build upon your awareness of Global Perspectives teaching and the pedagogical themes in this series.

Carr, M. (2009) *Differentiation Made Simple: Timesaving Tools for Teachers.* Austin: Prufrock Press.

Clarke, S. (2014) *Outstanding Formative Assessment: Culture and Practice.* London: Hodder Education.

Cottrell, S. (2011) *Critical Thinking Skills: Developing Effective Analysis and Argument (Palgrave Study Skills).* London: Palgrave Macmillan; 2nd edition.

Duke Writing Studio (2014) Online, *What Makes a Good Research Question?* The Duke Writing Studio website.

Gardner, H. (1993) *Multiple Intelligences: The Theory in Practice.* New York: Basic Books; Highlighting edition.

Edutopia for lesson ideas and strategies (2017) Online, the Edutopia website.

Gershon, M. (2013) *How to use Questioning in the Classroom: The Complete Guide: Volume 5* (How to … Great Classroom Teaching Series). CreateSpace Independent Publishing Platform.

Ginnis, P. (2002) *The Teacher's Toolkit: Raise Classroom Achievement with Strategies for Every Learner.* Crown House Publishing.

Griffiths, A. and Burns, M. (2012) *Outstanding Teaching: Engaging Learners* (Outstanding Teaching). Bancyfelin: Crown House Publishing.

Laycock, K. (2016) *Cambridge IGCSE® and O Level Global Perspectives Coursebook (Cambridge International IGCSE)*. Cambridge: Cambridge University Press.

Laycock, K. (2016) *Cambridge IGCSE® and O Level Global Perspectives Teacher's Resource CD-ROM (Cambridge International IGCSE)*. Cambridge: Cambridge University Press.

Moon, J. (2004) *A Handbook of Reflective and Experimental Learning*. London: Routledge Falmer.

Silberman, M. (1996) *Active Learning: 101 Strategies to Teach Any Subject*. London: Pearson.

Spiller, D. and Ferguson, P.B. (2011) Online, *Teaching Strategies to Promote the Development of Students' Learning Skills*. The University of Waikato website.

Stebbins, L. (2005) *Student Guide to Research in the Digital Age: How to Locate and Evaluate Information Sources*. Devon: Libraries Unlimited.

TrueTube, Online, the TrueTube website.

Watkins C (2015) *Meta-Learning in Classrooms*. The SAGE Handbook of Learning. Edited by Scott D. and Hargreaves E. London: Sage Publications Ltd.

Index

Printed in Great Britain
by Amazon

58047357R00086